HACKING WITH K

STEP BY STEP GUIDE TO LEARN KALI LINUX FOR HACKERS, CYBERSECURITY, WIRELESS NETWORK SECURITY AND PENETRATION TESTING. YOUR FIRST HACK AND COMPUTER HACKING BEGINNERS GUIDE.

licensed professional before attempting any techniques outlined in this book.

By reading this document, the reader agrees that under no circumstances is the author responsible for any losses, direct or indirect, which are incurred as a result of the use of information contained within this document, including, but not limited to, errors, omissions, or inaccuracies.

Introduction

Hackers work with the computer or program code, which is a set of instructions that work in the background and make up the software. While a lot of hackers do know how to program code, many downloads and use codes programmed by other people. The main requirement to know is how to work this code and adjust it to their advantage. For malicious hackers, that can be using it to steal passwords, secrets, identities, financial information, or create so much traffic that the targeted website needs to shut down.

Stealing passwords

Passwords are easy to hack because humans are very predictable. We think we are unique until it comes to passwords, but we are very easy to guess. For example, women will often use personal names for passwords—think kids, relatives, old flings—while men will stick to hobbies. The numbers we use most frequently are 1 and 2, and they are most often placed at the end of our password. More often than not, we use one word followed by some number, and if the website insists on including a capital letter, we place it at the beginning of the word and then whine about how this website is so annoying for making us go through all of this.

But how do hackers access our passwords? Well, there are several useful techniques.

The trial and error technique is called the brute force attack, and it is when you try possible combinations of letters and words to try and guess the right password. This can work because, as previously mentioned, we are very predictable when it comes to the type of passwords we use.

Another similar technique is called the dictionary attack; hackers use a file containing all the words that can be found in the dictionary, and the program tries them all. This is why it is often suggested to add numbers to your passwords as words, but this doesn't mean your "sunshine22" password is hackerproof.

A third technique is the rainbow table attack. The passwords in your computer system are hashed (generated into a value or values from a string of text using a mathematical function) in encryption. Whenever a user enters a password, it is compared to an already stored value, and if those match, you are able to enter

2

into the website or application. Since more text can produce the same value, it doesn't matter what letters we input as long as the encryption is the same. Think of it as a door and a key. You enter the doors with the key made for that lock, but if you're skilled at lock picking or a locksmith, you don't need that exact key to enter.

How to protect yourself from password attacks
Use the salt technique. This refers to adding simple random data to the input of a hash function. The process of combining a password with a salt which we then hash is called salting. For example, a password can be "sunshine22" but adding the salt is e34f8 (combining sunshine22 with e34f8) makes your hash-stored, new salted password "sunshine22e34f8." The new salted password is thus hashed into the system and saved into the database. Adding the salt just lowered the probability that the hash value will be found in any pre-calculated table. If you are a website owner, adding salt to each user's password creates a much more complicated and costly operation for hackers. They need to generate a pre-calculated table for each salted

password individually, making the process tedious and slow.

Even with the salt technique, determined hackers can pass through the "password salting." Another useful technique is the peppering technique. Just like the salt, pepper is a unique value. Pepper is different than salt because salt is unique for each user, but pepper is for everyone in the database. Pepper is not stored in the database; it's a secret value. Pepper means adding another extra value for storing passwords.

For example, let's say the pepper is the letter R. If the stored password is "sunshine22," the hash stored will be the hashed product of "sunshine22" with the added letter R. When the user logs, in the password they are giving is still "sunshine22," but the added pepper is storing "sunshine22" with the added R. The user has no knowledge that pepper is being used. The website will then cycle through every possible combination of peppers, and by taking upper and lowercase letters, there will be over 50 new combinations. The website will try hashing "sunshine22A," "sunshine22B," and so on until it reaches "sunshine22R." If one of the hashes matches the stored hash, then the user is allowed to log in. The whole point of this is that the pepper is not stored, so if the hacker wants to crack the password with a rainbow table or dictionary attack, it would take them over 50 times longer to crack a single password.

Phishing attacks

The easiest way to get someone's password is to ask them. After all, why bother with all the algorithms and cracking codes when you can just politely ask?

Phishing is often a promise of a prize if you click on a certain link that then takes you to a fake login page where you simply put in your password. The easiest way to defend from this is smart clicking, or not clicking on scammy pop-up ads.

Vacations and iPods are not just given away with a click and "you won't believe what happened next" is a sure sign of a clickbait leading to phishing.

Miracle weight loss pills, enlargement tools, singles waiting to meet you in the area and other promises of luxurious life with just one click are all phishing. Unfortunately, we have to work for money and workout for weight loss.

1. Hacking with Kali Linux

Kali Linux is an operating system that has many tools that are supposed to be utilized by security experts. There are more than 600 tools that have been pre-installed in the operating system. In this chapter, the main discussion will be about the Kali Linux for beginners. There are many people who may not be conversant with Kali Linux; however, in this chapter, it will be possible to learn how you can easily maneuver Kali Linux.

Kali Linux

The BackTrack platform was mainly formed for the security professionals and there are many tools that had been pre-installed in the Operating System. Since Kali Linux is the predecessor of the platform, the operating system also has many tools that can be utilized by the security professionals. The tools are mainly to be used by professionals such as network administrators and the security auditors. When using these tools, it is possible to assess the network and also ensure that it is secure. There are different types of hackers and they all have access to these tools.

BackTrack was useful to the security professionals, however, the main issue was that the architecture was quite complex and the tools that have been pre-installed could also not be used easily. The tools were present in the pentest directory and they were very effective when carrying out a penetration test. Many subfolders were also present and most of the tools could also be detected easily. The tools that were available in the platform include sqlninja- the tool comes in handy when carrying out SQL injection. Many more tools are also available and they can also be used to perform web exploitation when you are assessing the vulnerabilities that are present in the web applications.

Kali Linux replaced BackTrack and the architecture of the operating system is based on the Debian GNU, and it adheres to the Filesystem Hierarchy System (FHS) which also has many advantages as compared to the BackTrack platform. When you use the Kali Linux operating system, you can access the available tools easily since some of the applications can be located in the system path.

Kali Linux offers the following features:

- The operating system supports many desktop environments such as XFCE, Gnome, KDE, and LXDE. The operating system also offers some multilingual support.
- The tools offered by the operating system are Debian-compliant and they can also be synchronized at least four times daily using the Debian repositories. The packages can also be updated easily while also ensuring that some security fixes have also been applied.
- Kali Linux allows ISO customization and that means as a user, you can come up with different versions of Kali Linux that suit your needs.
- The operating system has both ARMEL and ARMFH support and that means that the users can also be able to install the Kali Linux operating system in different devices.
- The tools that have been pre-installed also have some diverse uses.
- Kali Linux is open source and that means it is free.

In this chapter, the main focus will be on the Kali Linux operating system as a virtual machine. For starters, the main focus will be on the Kali Linux for beginners to ensure that as a reader, you can get an overview of the operating system. To use an operating system as a virtual machine, you should utilize the VMware and that means that the Kali Linux operating system will be running on the "Live Mode."

There is a reason why the VMware is used and it is because it is easy to use and it comes in handy, especially when you execute different applications that are located in the primary operating system. For example, when you install the "Live Mode" on any operating system, you can use the applications that are present in the operating system. Additionally, you can retrieve the results that you have obtained when you carry out penetration testing using the virtual machine. The test results will allow you to learn about the vulnerabilities that are present in the system.

When you launch the Kali Linux operating system, the default desktop will appear and you will also notice that there is a menu bar as well as different icons. After selecting the menu item, you will be able to gain access to numerous security tools that have been pre-installed in the operating system.

How to Configure Secure Communications

When you use Kali Linux, you must ensure that there is connectivity to a wired or wireless network. After ensuring there is connectivity, the operating system will be able to handle various updates. Also, you can customize the operating system as long as there is connectivity. First, make sure there is an IP address. After that, confirm the IP address using the ifconfig command. You can confirm it using the terminal window and an example of the command being executed is as shown below:

In this case, the IP address is 192.168.204.132. At times, you may not be able to obtain the IP address and that means that you should use the dhclient eth0 command. The DHCP protocols will issue the IP address. Other interfaces can also be used to obtain the IP address and it will depend on the configurations that are present within the system.

When using a static IP address, you can also provide some additional information. For example, you can use the following IP address in such a manner:

After opening the terminal window, make sure that you have keyed in the following command:

Make sure that you have noted the changes that have been made to the IP settings. The changes will also not be persistent and they will not reappear after you have rebooted the operating system. In some instances, you may want to make sure that such changes are permanent. To do so, ensure that you have edited the /etc/network/interfaces file. The screenshot below can offer some subtle guidance:

When you start the Kali Linux operating system, the DHCP service will not be enabled. You are supposed to enable the DHCP service automatically. After enabling the service, the new IP addresses within the network will also be announced and the administrators will also receive an alert that there is an individual carrying out some tests.

Such an issue is not major; nonetheless, it is advantageous for some of the services start automatically in the process. Key in the following commands so that you may be able to achieve all this.

When using Kali Linux, you can also install varying network services including DHCP, HTTP, SSH, TFTP, and the VNC servers. The users can invoke these services straight from the command-line. Also, users can access these services from the Kali Linux menu.

Adjusting the Network Proxy Settings

Users can use proxies that are authenticated or unauthenticated and they can modify the proxy settings of the network using the bash.bashrc and apt.conf commands. The files will be present in this folder- /root/etc/directory.

1) Edit the bash.bashrc file first. A screenshot will be provided below since it will come in handy when offering some guidance. The text is also useful in such instances, especially if you want to add lines to the bash.bashrc file:

2) The proxy IP address will then be replaced with the Proxy IP address that you're using. Also, you will have administrator privileges and that means that you can also change the usernames and the

passwords. In some instances, you may also have to perform some authentication and you must key in the '@'symbol.

3) Create an apt.conf file in the same directory while also entering the commands that are showcased in the following screenshot:

4) Save the file and then close it. You can log in later so that you can activate the new settings.

Using Secure Shell to Secure Communications

As a security expert, you must ensure that the risk of being detected is minimized. With Kali Linux, you will not be able to use the external listening network devices. Some of the services that you can use are such as Secure Shell. First, install Secure Shell and then enable it so that you can use it.

The Kali Linux has some default SSH keys. Before starting the SSH service, disable the default keys first and also generate a keyset that is also unique since you may need it at some point. The default SSH keys will then be moved to the backup folder. To generate the SSH keyset.

To move the original keys, you should use the following command. Also, you can generate some new keysets using the same command.

Make sure that each of the keys has been verified. You can verify each key by calculating the md5sum hash values of every keyset. You can then compare the results that you have with the original keys.

When you start the SSH service, start with the menu and then select the Applications- Kali Linux- System Services-SSHD- SSHD start.

It is also possible to start the SSH when you are using the command line and this screenshot will guide you:

To verify that the SSH is running, execute the netstat query. The following screenshot will also guide you:

To stop the SSH, use this command:

Updating Kali Linux

For starters, the users must patch the Kali Linux operating system. The operating system must also be updated regularly so that it may also be up to date.

Looking into the Debian Package Management System

The package management system relies on the packages. The users can install and also remove packages as they wish when they are customizing the operating system. The packages support different tasks such as penetration testing. Users can also extend the functionality of the Kali Linux such that the operating system can support communications and documentation. As for the documentation process, run the wine application so that you can run applications such as the Microsoft Office. Some of the packages will also be stored in the repositories.

Packages and Repositories

With Kali Linux, you can only use the repositories provided by the operating system. If the installation process has not been completed, you may not be able to add the repositories. Different tools are also present on the operating system, although they may not be present in the official tool repositories. The tools may be updated manually and you should overwrite the packaged files that are present and the dependencies should also be present. The Bleeding Edge repository can also maintain various tools including Aircrack-ng, dnsrecon, sqlmap, and beef-xss. You should also note that it is impossible to move some of these tools from their respective repositories to the Debian repositories. The Bleeding Edge repository can be added to the sources. List using this command: *Dpkg*

This is a package management system that is also based on Debian. It is possible to remove, query, and also installs different packages when you are using the command-line application. After triggering the dpkg-1, some data will be returned in the process. In the process, you can also view all the applications that have been pre-installed into the Kali Linux operating system. To access some of the applications, you should make use of the command line.

Using Advanced Packaging Tools

The Advanced Packing Tools (APT) is essential when you are extending the dpkg functionally when searching and installing the repositories. Some of the packages may also be upgraded. The APT comes in handy when a user wants to upgrade the whole distribution.

The common APT (Advanced Packaging Tools) is as follows:

- *Apt-Get Upgrade* - This is a command that is used to install the latest versions of various packages that have been installed on Kali Linux. Some of these packages have also been installed on Kali Linux and it is also possible to upgrade them. If there are no packages present, you cannot upgrade anything. Only installed packages can be upgraded.
- *Apt-Get Update* - This is a command that is used when resynchronizing the local packages with each of their sources. Ensure that you are using the update command when performing the upgrade.
- *Apt-Get Dist-Upgrade* - The command upgrades all the packages that are already installed in the system. The packages that are obsolete should also be removed.

To view all the full descriptions of some of the packages, you should use the apt-get command. It is also possible to identify the dependencies of each package. You may also remove the packages using various commands. Also, it is good to note that some packages may also not be removed using the apt-get command. You should update some packages manually using the update.sh script and you should also use the commands that are shown below:

Customizing and Configuring Kali Linux

The Kali Linux operating system framework is quite useful when performing penetration tests. As a security expert, you will not be limited to using the tools that have been pre-installed in Kali Linux. It is also possible to adjust the default desktop on Kali Linux. After customizing Kali Linux, you can also make sure that the system is more secure. After collecting some data, it will also be safe and the penetration test can also be carried out easily.

The common customizations include:

- You can reset the root password.
- You can add a non-root user.
- Share some folders with other operating systems such as Microsoft Windows.
- Creating folders that are encrypted.
- Speeding up the operations at Kali Linux.

Resetting the Root Password

Use the following command so that you can change the root password:

Key in the new password. The following screenshot will guide you:

How to Add a Non-Root User

There are many applications that are provided by Kali Linux and they usually run as long as the user has the root-level privileges. The only issue is that the root-level privileges have some risks and they may include damaging some applications when you use the wrong commands when testing different systems. When testing a system, it is advisable to use user-level privileges. You may create a non-root user when using the adduser command. Start by keying in the following command in the terminal window. This screenshot will guide you:

How to Speed Up the Operations on Kali Linux

You can use different tools to speed up the processes in Kali Linux:

- When creating the virtual machine, ensure that the disk size is fixed and that way it will be faster as compared to a disk that is allocated in a dynamic manner. As for the fixed disk, it will be easy to add files fast and the fragmentation will be less.

- When using the virtual machine, make sure that you have installed the VMware tools.
- To delete the cookies and free up some space on the hard disk, use the BleachBit application. To ensure that there is more privacy, ensure that the cache has been cleared as well as the browsing history. There are some advanced features such as shredding files and also wiping the disk space that is free. There are some traces that cannot also be fully deleted since they are hidden.
- Preload applications exist and they can also be used to identify different programs that are also used commonly by various users. Using these applications, you can preload the binaries and the dependencies onto the memory and that will ensure that there is faster access. Such an application will also work automatically after ensuring that the installation process is complete.
- Although Kali Linux has many tools, they are not all present on the start-up menu. The

system data will also slow down when an application has been installed during the start-up process and the memory use shall also be impacted. The unnecessary services and applications should also be disabled; to do so, make sure you have installed the Boot up Manager (BUM). This screenshot will guide you:

- You can also launch a variety of applications directly from the keyboard and make sure that you have added gnome-do so that you can access different applications from the accessories menu. After that, you will launch gnome-do and select the preferences menu and also activate the Quite Launch function afterward. Select the launch command and then clear all existing commands and enter the command line so that you can execute different commands after you have launched the selected keys.

Some of the applications can also be launched using various scripts.

Sharing the Folders with Another OS

Kali Linux has numerous tools. The operating system is also suitable since it offers some flexibility with regard to the applications that have already been pre-installed. To access the data that is present in Kali Linux and the host operating system, make sure that you are using the "Live Mode." You will then create a folder that you can also access easily.

The important data will be saved in that folder and you will then access it from either of the operating systems. The following steps will guide you on how to create a folder:

1) Create the folder on the operating system. For example, will be issued in the form of a screenshot, the folder, in this case, is named "Kali."

2) Right-click the "Kali" folder. You will then click 'share.'

3) Ensure that the file is shared with 'everyone'. People can also read and write an

4) My content is present in the "Kali" folder.

5) You can also install some VMware tools of you have not yet shared and created the folder.

6) After the installation process is complete, select the virtual machine setting. It will be present in the VMware menu. You will then share the folders and make sure that you have selected enabled. You will then create a path that allows you to select shared folders that are located in the primary operating system.

7) Open the browser that is present on the Kali Linux default desktop. The shared folder will be present in the mint folder.

8) Ensure that the folder has been dragged to the Kali Linux desktop.

9) Make sure that all the information that has been placed into the folder is also accessible from the main operating system and Kali Linux.

When undertaking a pen test, make sure that you have stored all the findings in the shared folder. The information that you have gathered may be sensitive and you must ensure that it is encrypted. You can encrypt the information in different ways. For example, you can use LVM encryption. You can encrypt a folder or even an entire partition on the hard disk. Make sure that you can remember the password since you will not be able to reset it in case your memory fails you. If you fail to remember the password, the data will be lost in the process. It is good to encrypt the folders so that the data may not be accessed by unauthorized individuals.

Managing Third-Party Applications

Kali Linux has many applications and they are normally pre-installed. You may also install other applications on the platform but you need to make sure that they are from verifiable sources. Since Kali Linux is meant for penetration testing, some of the tools that are present on the platform are quite advanced. Before using these applications, make sure that you understand them fully so that you can use them effectively. You can also locate different applications easily.

Installing Third-Party Applications

There are many techniques that you can use when installing third-party applications. The commonly used techniques are such as the use of apt-get command and it is useful when accessing different repositories including GitHub and also installing different applications directly.

When you install different applications, make sure that they are all present in the Kali Linux repository. Use the apt-get install command during the installation process. The commands should be executed in the terminal window. During the installation process, you will also realize that the graphical package management tools will come in handy.

You can install different third-party applications and some of them include:

- *Gnome-Tweak-Tool* - This is a tool that normally allows the users to configure some desktop options and the user can also change the themes easily. The desktop screen recorder will also allow you to record different activities that may be taking place on the desktop.
- *Apt-File* - This is a command that is used to search for different packages that may be present within the APT packaging system. When using this command, you can list the contents of different packages prior to installing them.
- *Scrub* - The tool is used to delete data securely and it also complies with various government standards.

- *Open office* - This application offers users the productivity suite that will be useful during the documentation.
- *Team Viewer* - This tool ensures that people can have remote access. The penetration testers can use the tool to carry out the penetration test from a remote location.
- *Shutter* - Using this tool, you can take screenshots on the Kali Linux platform.
- *Terminator* - The tool allows users to scroll horizontally.

There are numerous tools that are not available in the Debian repository and they can also be accessed using various commands such as apt-get install command which can also be installed on the Kali Linux platform. Users should first learn that the manual installation techniques involve the use of repositories and it is also possible to break down the dependencies which means that some of the applications may also fail in the process.

The GitHub repository has many tools and they are used mainly by the software developers when handling different projects. Some of the developers will prefer to utilize open repositories since they will gain a lot of flexibility. Different applications should also be installed manually. Make sure that you have also perused through the README file since it provides some guidance on how to use some of these tools.

Running the Third-Party Applications Using Non-Root Privileges

Kali Linux supports different activities such as penetration testing. There are some tools that can only run when a user has root-level access. Some of the data and tools may also be [protected using password and different encryption techniques. There are some tools that you can also run using the non-root privileges. Some of these tools are such as web browsers.

After compromising tools such as web browsers, the attackers will have some root privileges. To run applications as a non-root user, you should log in to Kali Linux first while using the root account. Ensure that the Kali Linux has been configured using a non-root account after that. An example will be provided whereby a non-root user account was formulated using the add user command.

The steps that you should follow are outlined below. In this instance, we will run the Iceweasel browser and we will use the non-root Kali Linux user account.

1. Create a non-root user account.
2. We will use the sux application. The application is used when transferring different credentials from the root user account to the non-root user. When installing the application, use the apt-get install command.
3. You can launch the web browser and you should minimize it after that.
4. Use this command: ps aux | grep Iceweasel. In this case, you will be running the browser using the root privileges.
5. Close the browser and then start it all over again. Use the sux- noroot Iceweasel command to relaunch the application. The screenshot below will offer some subtle guidance.

Examine the browser title bar and you will realize that the browser was run as a non-root user and no administrator privileges are present.

Observe all the open processes after ensuring that the browser is running under the noroot account.

Effectively Managing the Penetration Tests

When you perform the penetration tests, you will come across a series of challenges and every test will also be carried out to unveil different vulnerabilities that may be present within the network or server. In some instances, you may not remember that you had conducted some tests and you may also be unable to keep track of the tests that you had already completed.

Some of the penetration tests are quite complex and the methodology used must adapt to that of the target. There are many applications that may be used when performing the tests and they include keyloggers and also Wireshark, just to mention a few. Each application is used when performing specific tests. The data that is gathered using these applications comes in handy. After the packets have been analyzed, it is easy to identify the packet tools that may have been affected.

There are many tools that are present in Kali Linux and some of them can also be used to make some rapid notes while serving as repositories using the KeepNote desktop wiki and Zim. Testers will also be able to carry out a variety of tests. In the process, they will collect some data that will also be used to facilitate the tests.

The tests help to identify some of the changes that have taken place in the system. Some vulnerabilities may emerge and they should be sealed immediately to ensure that external attackers will not be able to access the system and gain access to sensitive pieces of information. As a tester, make sure that you have collected some evidence in the form of screenshots and you can present your findings to the clients while explaining to them about some of the vulnerabilities that are present in the network. Use tools such as shutter to take screenshots. You can also use CutyCapt and it will save the images in a variety of formats.

2. Back Door Attacks

Imagine you're going to a concert, but you don't have a ticket. You see the line of people all with their purchased tickets waiting to get through security. You see cameras pointing at the front door and a few extra security guards guarding the sides. You don't have a ticket or the money to buy one. Then, you see a little unguarded, dark, hidden alley with no cameras and the back door. The doors that lead to the venue. They are unlocked, and there are no security or cameras around. Would you go through the door? That's the concept behind a back-door attack.

How do backdoors even end up on our computers? Well, they can end up there intentionally by the manufacturer; this is built in so they can easily test out the bugs and quickly move in the applications as they are being tested.

The back door can also be built by malware. The classic backdoor malware is the infamous Trojan. Trojan subtly sneaks up on our computer and opens the back door for the people using the malware. The malware can be hidden into anything—a free file converter, a PDF file, a torrent, or anything you are downloading into your computer. Of course, the chances are higher when what you're downloading is a free copy of an otherwise paid product (lesson to be learned here). Trojans have an ability to replicate, and before you know it, your computer is infected with malware that is opening a backdoor for the whole line up to come in to see the show for free.

The back door can be used to infiltrate your system not only for passwords but also for spying, ransomware, and all kinds of other malicious hacking.

How to protect yourself from back door attacks
Choose applications, downloads and plugins carefully; free apps and plugins are a fantastic thing, but YouTube to MP3 converters, torrents of the latest Game of Thrones season, and a copy of Photoshop might not be the best option if you're interested in keeping your passwords safe. Android users should stick to Google Play apps, and Mac users should stick with the Apple store. Track app permissions too and be sure to read, at least a little, before you sign your life away to a third-grade flashlight application.

You can also try:

Monitoring network activity - Use firewalls and track your data usage. Any data usage spike is a sure sign of backdoor activity.

Changing your default passwords - When a website assigns a default password, we may find that we are just too lazy to take the 30 seconds necessary to change it. Just do it. You might not be locking the back door with the latest state-of-the-art security system, but at least you are not keeping them wide open with a neon sign pointing to your password. Freckles might be your puppy, but he can't be a password for everything. A common complaint is, "I will forget it." Write it down. Contrary to popular belief, hackers won't go into your house and search for that piece of paper, but they will go into your computer. Which option seems safer?

Zombie Computers for Distributed Denial of Service (DDoS) attacks

Sounds extremely cool, right? Well, it's not. Basically, a computer becomes a zombie computer when a hacker infiltrates it and controls it to do illegal activities. The best part (for the hacker, not for you) is that you are completely unaware that all this is happening. You will still use it normally, though it might significantly slow down. And then all of a sudden, your computer will begin to send out massive spam emails or social media posts that you have nothing to do with. DDoS attacks are lovely (for the hacker, not for you) because they work on multiple computers at once, and the numbers can go into millions. A million zombie computers are mindlessly wandering around the internet spamming everything in sight, infecting other computers. The version where your computer is infected only to send out spam is the light version. DDoS attacks can also be used for criminal activity, and this is why it is important to prevent them.

How to protect from DDoS attacks

Larger scale businesses require more substantial protection against DDoS attacks, and we will go over that in detail, but even for individuals, half of the protection is prevention.

Understand the warning signs—slowed down computers, spotty connection, or website shutdowns are all signs of a DDoS attack taking place.

What can you do?

Have more bandwidth - This ensures you have enough bandwidth to deal with massive spikes in traffic that can be caused by malicious activity

Use anti-DDoS hardware and software modules - Protect your servers with network and web application firewalls. Hardware vendors can add software protection by monitoring how incomplete connections and specific software modules can be added to the webserver software to provide DDoS protection.

Smart clicking - This should go without saying, but for those in need of hearing it—pop-up ads with a "No, thanks" button are hateful little things. Just exit the website, don't click anything on that ad, especially not the "No, thanks," button or you will instantly activate an annoying download, and now your computer is a zombie.

Man in The Middle

When you're online, your computer does little back-and-forth transactions. You click a link, and your computer lets the servers around the world know you are requesting access to this website. The servers then receive the message and grant you access to the requested website. This all happens in nanoseconds, and we don't think much about it. That nanosecond moment between your computer and the web server is given a session ID that is unique and private to your computer and the webserver. However, a hacker can hijack this session and pretend to be the computer and as such, gain access to usernames and passwords. He becomes the man in the middle hijacking your sessions for information.

How to protect yourself from the man in the middle

Efficient antivirus and up-to-date software go a long way in preventing hijacking, but there are a couple of other tips that can help you prevent becoming a victim.

Use a virtual private network - A VPN is a private, encrypted network that acts as a private tunnel and severely limits the hacker's access to your information. Express VPN can also mask your location, allowing you to surf the web anonymously wherever you are.

Firewalls and penetration testing tools - Secure your network with active firewalls and penetration testing tools.

Plugins - Use only trusted plugins from credible sources and with good ratings.

Secure your communications - Use two-step verification programs and alerts when someone signs in to your account from a different computer.

Root Access

Root access is an authorization to access any command specific to Unix, Linux, and Linux-like systems. This gives the hacker complete control over the system. Root access is granted with a well-designed rootkit software. A quality designed rootkit software will access everything and hide traces of any presence. This is possible in all Unix-like systems because they are designed with a tree-like structure in which all the units branch off into one root.

The original Unix operating system was designed in a time before the personal computer existed when all the computers were connected to one mainframe computer through very simple terminals. It was necessary to have one large, strong mainframe for separating and protecting files while the users simultaneously used the system.

Hackers obtain root access by gaining privileged access with a rootkit. Access can be granted through passwords; password protection is a significant component in restricting unwanted root access. The rootkit can also be installed automatically through a malicious download. Dealing with rootkit can be difficult and expensive, so it's better to stay protected and keep the possibility of root access attacks to the minimum.

How to protect yourself from root access attacks
Quality antivirus software is one of the standard things recommended in all computers, be it for individuals or businesses. Quality antivirus helps the system hardening making it harder for installation of rootkits.

Principle of least privilege - PoLP gives only the bare minimum privilege that a program needs to perform allows for better protection from possible attacks. For example, in a business, a user whose only job is to answer emails should only be given access to the emails. If there is an attack on the user's computer, it can't spread far because the person only has access to email. If a said employee has root access privilege, the attack will spread system-wide.

Disable root login - Servers on most Unix and Linux operating systems come with an option for the root login. Using root login allows for much easier root access, and if you pair it with a weak password, you are walking on a thin line. Disabling the option for root access keeps all the users away from the root login temptation.

Block brute forces - Some programs will block suspicious IP addresses for you. They will detect malicious IP and prevent attacks. While manually detecting is the safest way, it can be a long process; programs that are designed to block malicious IPs can drastically save time and help prevent root access attacks.

The best way to protect yourself from hack attacks is through prevention because the alternative can be lengthy, exhausting, and costly.

3. Cybersecurity

The internet is a vast place, and most people are not experts on protecting the information about them that is available. It's no surprise that there are people out there who take advantage of others' ignorance. But there are ways to protect yourself from those kinds of attacks, and that's where cybersecurity comes in.

What is Cybersecurity?

By the time you finish reading this sentence, over 300 million people will have clicked on a single link. You are part of a universe that generates information every millisecond. We do everything from home—buy, sell, eat, drink, fight, tweet, click, and share. We don't need to go to the movies to see a movie or go to the stores to shop. Information exchanges happen online every time you connect to Wi-Fi, publish content, buy something online, like a post on social media, click a link, send an email...you get the gist. We produce much more information than we can grasp, so we underestimate the quantity and value of protecting it.

Cybersecurity is the protection of hardware, software, and data from cyberattacks. Cybersecurity ensures data confidentiality, availability, and integrity. A successful and secure system has multiple layers of protection spread across the networks, computers, data, and programs. For cybersecurity to be effective, all the people involved in different components must complement each other. It is always better to prevent cyberattacks then deal with the consequences of one.

Cyberattacks hit businesses every day. The latest statistics show that hackers now focus more on quieter attacks, but they are increased by over 50%.

During 2018, 1% of websites were considered victims of cyberattacks. Thinking about 1% of all websites that exist, that adds up to over 17 million websites that are always under attack. Cyberattacks cost an average of $11 million per year, so cybersecurity is a crucial aspect of saving your business much money.

That's where the most prominent problem occurs. Small business owners and individuals don't grasp the potential threat to their data because they don't see the value they bring to a hacker attacking. The value is in the lack of security.

Many small businesses with no security are more accessible to penetrate than one large corporation. Corporations invest in cybersecurity; small business owners and individuals do not. They use things like the cloud. Their data migrate with them to the cloud allowing criminals to shift and adapt. The lack of security on their part is crucial to these statistics. The most definite form of on-going attacks remains ransomware; it is so common-place that it is barely even mentioned in the media. Ransomware infects a website by blocking access to their data until a business or an individual transfer a certain amount of money. Hackers hold your data hostage, and it's always about the money.

Cybersecurity is not complicated, it is complex. However, it is also very important to understand. Implementing just the top four cybersecurity strategies diminishes attacks by over 70%. Here are some of the techniques:

Application whitelisting - allowing only approved programs to run

Applications security patching - enforcing security patches (fixes) promptly for applications

Operating systems security patching - enforcing security patches (fixes) promptly for the whole system

Limiting administrative privileges - allowing only trusted individuals to manage and monitor computer systems

Cybersecurity Benefits

There's a variety of benefits cybersecurity can bring to you or your business, and some aren't as obvious as you may think.

Prevents ransomware - Every 10 seconds, someone becomes a victim of ransomware. If you don't know what is happening in your network, an attacker probably found a way to get into it.

Prevents adware - Adware fills your computer with ads and allows the attacker to get into your network.

Prevents spyware - The attacker can spy on your activity and use that information to learn about your computer and network vulnerabilities

Improves your search engine rankings - SEO is the key in the modern digital market. Small businesses looking to rank up on search engines have to be educated in

SEO if they want to advance financially. HTTPS (HyperText Transfer Protocol Secure), or the encryption of username, passwords, and information, is one of the critical SEO ranking factors.

Prevents financial loss and saves your startup - More than half of small business go down after a cyberattack. The downtime required to fix the damage prevents any new business, and the data breach causes you to lose the trust of your current customers. Stable businesses can find a way to recover from this, but startups rarely make it out alive.

4. Wireless Networking

While talking about networking, one of the most trending topics is wireless networking. It has allowed people to reach new heights of reliability along with benefits which allow them to use the internet with their devices without any form of cable or wire in between. All of these have been possible only because of wireless networking. In wireless networking, all the devices connect with a network switch or router which helps in establishing connection between the devices and the Web via radio waves. All the information and connection are established through the air. Thus, it can be regarded as a mobile form of network where you are no longer required to be seated in one single place for surfing the internet. Wireless networking comes with various components along with some very interesting features which will be discussed further in this chapter. So, let's start with wireless networking and its various features.

Hacking and Penetration Testing with Kali Linux

Each and every organization and companies come with certain weak points which might turn out to be malicious for the organization. Such weak points can also lead to some serious form of attack which can be later used for manipulation of organizational data. The only thing that you are left with in such a situation which can ultimately help you in preventing all forms of hackers from getting into your systems is regular checking of infrastructure security. You will also need to ensure that no form of vulnerability is present within the infrastructure. For serving all of these functions, penetration testing is something which can ultimately help you. It helps in detecting the vulnerabilities within a system and forwards the same information to the organization administrators for mending up the gaps. Penetration testing is always performed within a highly secure and real form of environment which helps in finding out the real form of vulnerabilities and then mends the following along with securing the system.

Details about penetration testing

It is a process which is used for testing of the systems for finding out or ensuring that whether any third party can penetrate within the system or not. Ethical hacking is often being mixed up with penetration testing as both of them somewhat serves the similar purpose and also functions more or less in the same way. In penetration testing, the pen tester scans the systems for any form of system vulnerability, flaws, risks and malicious content. You can perform penetration testing either in an online form of environment or server or even in a computer system. Penetration testing comes with some ultimate form of agendas: strengthening the system of security and defending the structure of an organization from potential attacks and threats.

Penetration testing is absolutely of legal nature and is done along with the other official workings. When used in the proper and perfect way, penetration testing has the ability of doing wonders. If you want you can also consider penetration testing as a potential part of ethical hacking. You will need to perform the penetration tests at a regular form of intervals as it has the ability of improving the system capabilities. It also helps in improving the cyber security strategies. In order to fish out all the weak points within a program, system or application, various forms of malicious content are constructed or created by the pen testers. For an effective form of testing, the harmful form of content is spread across the overall network for the testing of vulnerability.

The technique used by penetration testing might not be successful in handling all the security concerns but it can help to minimize the chances of probable attacks on the system. Penetration testing ensures that an organization or company is absolutely safe from all forms of threats and vulnerabilities and it ultimately helps in providing security from the cyber form of attacks. It also makes sure that the system of defense of an organization is working properly and is also enough for the company or organization to prevent the probable attacks and threats. Not only that but it also indicates the measures of security which are required to be changed by the organization for the only motive of defending the system from attacks and vulnerabilities. All the reports regarding penetration testing are handed over to the system administrators.

Metasploit

Metasploit is nothing but a framework meant for penetration testing which actually makes the concept of hacking much simpler and easier. It is regarded as an important form of tool for majority of the attackers along with the security defenders. All you need to do is to just point out Metasploit at the target, pick any exploit of your choice, choose the payload which you want to drop and just hit enter. However, it is not that casual in nature and so you will need to start from the beginning. Back in the golden days, the concept of penetration testing came with lots of repetitive form of labor which is now being automated by the use of Metasploit.

What are the things that you need? Gathering of information or gaining of access or maintaining the levels of persistence or evading all forms f detection? Metasploit can be regarded as the Swiss knife for the hackers and if you want to opt for information security as your future career then you are required to know this framework in detail. The core of the Metasploit framework is free in nature and also comes pre-installed with the software Kali Linux.

How to use Metasploit?

Metasploit can seamlessly integrate itself with SNMP scanning, Nmap and enumeration of Windows patch along with others. It also comes with a bridge to the

Tenable's scanner of vulnerability along with Nessus. Most of the reconnaissance tools which you can think of can integrate along with Metasploit and thus it makes it possible to find the strongest possible point in the shield of security. After you have identified the weakness in a system, you can start hunting across the huge and extensible form of database for the need of the exploit which will help in cracking the strongest armor and will let you in the system. Just like the combination of cheese and wine, you can also pair an exploit with the payload for suiting any task at the hand.

Most of the hackers are looking out for a shell, a proper payload at the time of attacking a system based on Windows acts as the Meterpreter and also as an in-memory form of interactive shell. Linux comes with its own set of shellcodes which depends on the exploit which is being used. Once within a target machine, the quiver of Metasploit comes with a complete suite of post-exploitation tools which also includes escalation of privileges, pass the hash, screen capture, packet sniffing, pivoting and keylogger tools. If you want you can also easily set up a proper form of backdoor if the target machine gets rebooted somehow.

Metasploit is being loaded up with more and more features each year along with a fuzzer for identifying the potential flaws of security in the binaries as well as a too long list of the modules which are of auxiliary nature. What we have discussed till now is only a high-level vision of what can be done with Metasploit. The overall framework is modular in nature and can be extended easily and it also enjoys an active form of community. In case it is not doing what you want, you can easily tweak the same for meeting your needs.

How can you learn Metasploit?

You can find out various cheap as well as free forms of resources for the purpose of learning Metasploit. The best way of starting with Metasploit is by downloading Kali Linux followed by the installation of the same along with a virtual machine for practicing of the target. The organization which maintains Kali Linux and also runs the OSCP certification, Offensive Security, offers a free course that includes training of Metasploit and is known as Metasploit Unleashed.

Where can you download Metasploit?

Metasploit can be found along with the hacking software Kali Linux. But, if you want you can also download it separately from the official website of Metasploit. Metasploit can be used on the systems which are based on Windows and *nix. You can find out the source code of Metasploit Framework on GitHub. Metasploit is also available in various forms which you can easily find over the internet.

Datastore

The datastore can be regarded as a core element of the Metasploit Framework. It is nothing but a table of several named values which allows the users to easily configure the component behavior within Metasploit. The datastore allows the interfaces to configure any of the settings, exploits for defining the parameters and also payloads for the purpose of patching the opcodes. It also allows Metasploit Framework to pass internally between the options of modules. You can find two types of datastores, the Global datstore which can be defined by using 'setg' and the Module datastore which can be defined at the modular level of datastore by using 'set'.

SQL Injection and Wi-Fi Hacking

When it comes to cyber-attacks one of the most widely used forms of attack is the SQL Injection attack. In this, an attacker performs the attack by executing threat or invalid form of SQL statements which is used for database server control for an application of web. It is also being used for modifying, deleting or adding up records within the database without even the user knowing anything about the same. This ultimately compromises the integrity of the data. The most important step which can be taken for avoiding or preventing SQL injection is by input validation.

SQL Injection and its types

There are various types of SQL injection which you can find today. Let's have a look at them.

- Classic or In-band SQL injection: 1. Error based: Attackers employ the generated error by the database to attack the database server.

2. Union based: In this UNION SQL operator is employed for combining a response for returning to the HTTP response.

- Inferential or Blind SQL injection: 1. Based on Boolean: It is based on return of true or false.

2. Time based: It sends out SQL injection which forces the database just before responding.

- Out of band SQL injection: This takes place when an attacker is unable to use the similar form of channel for attacking and gathering the results.

Tools used for SQL injection

There are various tools which are being used for carrying out SQL injection.

- SQLMap: This tool is used for an automatic form of SQL injection and it is a tool which helps in taking over the database.

- jSQL Injection: It is a Java based tool which is being used for SQL injection.

- Blind-SQL-BitShifting: It is a tool which is used for blind SQL injection by the use of BitShifting.

- BBQSQL: It is a blind form of SQL injection exploitation tool.

- explo: It is a format of machine and human readable web vulnerability testing.

- Whitewidow: It is a scanning tool which is used for checking out the vulnerabilities of the SQL database.

- Leviathan: It acts as an audio toolkit.

- Blisqy: It is used for the purpose of exploiting time-based SQL injection within the headers of HTTP.

Detection tools for SQL injection

A tool named Spider testing tool is widely being used for the purpose of identifying the holes of SQL injection manually by the use of POST or GET requests. If you can resolve the vulnerabilities within the code then you can easily prevent the SQL injections. You can also take help of a web vulnerability scanner for identifying all the defects within the code and for fixing the same f0r preventing SQL injection. The firewalls present in the web application or within the application layer can also be used extensively for preventing any form of intrusion.

Hacking of Wi-Fi

Wi-Fi or wireless networking can be regarded as the most preferred medium which is being used for the purpose of network connectivity in today's world. However, because of so much popularity of the same, the wireless networks are also subjected to various attacks and also comes with several issues of security. In case the attacker gains complete access of the network connection then it is possible for the attacker to sniff off the data packets from any nearby location. The attackers employ sniffing tools for finding out the SSIDs and then hacks the Wi-Fi or wireless networks. After successful hacking, the attackers can monitor all the devices which are connected with the same SSID of the network. In case you use authentication of WEP then it might be subject to dictionary attack. The attackers employ RC4 form of encryption algorithm for the purpose of creating stream ciphers which is very easy to be cracked. In case you are using authentication of WPA then it might subject to DOS along with dictionary attack.

Tools for hacking of Wi-Fi

For the purpose of cracking WEP, the attackers use various tools such as WEPcrack, Aircrack, Kismet, WEPDecrypt and many others. For cracking WPA, tools such as Cain, Abel and CowPatty are being used by the hackers. There are also various types of tools which are used in general for hacking of wireless network system like wireshark, Airsnort, Wifiphisher, Netstumbler and many others. Even the attackers are now able to hack the mobile phone platform via the wireless network system. Android can be regarded as the most found mobile phone-based platform but it is also very much susceptible to some specific types of vulnerabilities which ultimately makes it easier for the attackers to exploit the device security and then steal data from the same. The most dangerous threats for the mobile devices are third party applications, email Trojans, wireless hacking and SMS.

How are Wi-Fi attacks carried out?

Most of the wireless network attacks are carries out by setting up rogue Access Point.

- *Evil Twin attack:* In this, the hacker sets up a false access point with the same name as that of the corporate AP which is close to the premises of the company. When any employee of the company connects to that access point by regarding that access point to be genuine in nature, that employee unknowingly gives out all the details of authentication of the actual access point. Thus, the hacker can easily compromise the overall connection.

- *Signal jamming:* The hackers can easily disrupt the network connection which can be done by jamming the network signals. This is done by various forms of tools which are used for creating noise.

- *Misconfiguration attack:* When the router of a network is set up by using a default form of configuration, weak form of encryption, weak credentials and algorithms, an attacker can easily crack the network.

- *Honey spot attack:* The attackers set up false hotspots or access points with the same name of the SSID similar to any public Wi-Fi access point. When any user connects with that access point unknowingly, the hackers can easily get access to the actual network.

How To Carry Out An Effective Attack

When it comes to the term 'hacking' it doesn't mean that it has to be negative all the time. You will be able to have a proper idea about the overall process of hacking only when you will have a clear perception about the process behind it. Not only that you will be able to gather knowledge about the process of hacking but you will also be able to make your system much more protected from external attacks. Most of the times, when an attacker tries to gain access to a server of an organization or a company, it is generally done by using 5 proper steps. Let's have a look at those steps.

• Reconnaissance: This can be regarded as the very first step that comes in the hacking process. During this phase, the attacker uses all the available means for the purpose of collecting all forms of relevant information about the primary target system. The relevant set of information might include the proper identification of the target, DNS records of the server, range of the IP address which is in target, the network and various other aspects. In simple terms, the attacker tries to collect all sorts of information along with the contacts of a website or server. This can be done by the attacker by the use of several forms of search engines like maltego or by researching about the system which is in target or by using the various tools like HTTPTrack for the purpose of downloading a complete website for enumeration at a later stage.

By performing all these steps, the attacker will be able to determine the names of all the staffs within an organization very easily, find out the designated posts along with the email addresses of the employees.

• Scanning: After collecting all the relevant information about the target, the attacker will now start with the process of scanning. During this phase, the attacker employs various forms of tools like dialers, port scanners, vulnerability scanners, sweepers and network mappers for the sole purpose of scanning the target website or server data. During this step, the attackers try to seek out all that information which can actually help in the execution of a successful attack such as the IP address of the system, the user accounts and the computer names within that server. Right after the hackers are done with scanning of basic information, they start to test the network which is in target for finding out the possible avenues of attack. They might also employ several methods for network mapping just like Kali Linux.

The hackers also search out for any automatic email system by which they can mail out the staffs of the target company about some false form of query like mailing the company HR about a job query.

• Access gaining: This is the most important of all the steps. In this phase, the attacker designs out the blueprint of the target network along with the help of all relevant information which is also collected in the first and second step of hacking. As the hackers are done with enumeration of data followed by scanning of the system, they will now move to the step of gaining access to the system which will be based on the collected information.

For instance, the attacker might decide to use a phishing attack. The attackers will always try to play safe and might employ a very simple attack of phishing for gaining overall access to the system. The attacker might also penetrate into the system from the IT department shell. The hackers use phishing email by employing the actual email address of the company. By using this phishing email ID, the attacker will send out various emails to the techs that will also contain some form of specialized program along with a phishing website for gathering information about the login passwords and IDs. For this, the attackers can use various methods such as phone app, website mail or something else and then asking the employees to login with their credentials into a new website.

As the hackers use this method, they already have a special type of program running in the background which is also called as Social Engineering Toolkit which is used for sending out emails with the address of the server to the users.

- Maintaining access to the server: After the attackers have gained access to the target server, they will try out every possible means for keeping their access to the server safe for future attacks and for the purpose of exploitation. As the attacker now has overall access to the server, he might also use the server as his very own base for launching out several other forms of attacks. When an attacker gains access to an overall system and also owns the system, such a system is called as zombie system. The hacker might also try to hide himself within the server by creating a new administrator account with which he can easily mingle with the system without anyone knowing about it. For keeping safe access to the system, the hacker traces out all those accounts which are not being used for a long time and then elevates the privileges of all those accounts to himself.

As the hacker makes sure that no one has sensed his presence within the system, he starts to make copies of all the data on that server along with the contacts, messages, confidential files and many more for future use.

- Clearance of tracks: Right before starting with the attack, the hackers chalk out their entire track regarding the identity so that it is not possible for anyone to track them. The attackers begin by altering the system MAC address and then run their entire system via a VPN so that no one can trace their actual identity.

5. How to Initiate A Hack Using Kali Linux?

When planning an attack, the most important factor to consider is the pilot study. It should come first before you carry out an attack or a penetration test on a target. As an attacker, you will have to dedicate a lot of time to the reconnaissance. In this stage, the attacker will be able to define, map, and also explore some of the vulnerabilities that are present and they will be able to successfully perform an exploit. There are two types of pilot studies; passive and active.

The passive pilot study involves the analysis of the information that is available. For instance, some information can be obtained online through search engines. The information can be analyzed first. Although an attacker can use this information to their advantage, it is not possible to trace the information back to them. As for passive reconnaissance, it is mainly carried out to ensure that the target cannot easily notice that there is a looming attack.

The major practices and principles of the passive reconnaissance include:

OSINT (Open-source intelligence).

How to obtain user information.

The basics of the pilot study.

The Basic Principles of the Pilot Study

The pilot study is the first step when a person wants to launch an attack. The study is carried out after identifying a target. The information that is gained during this stage will come in handy when performing the actual attack. A reconnaissance will ensure that they have provided a sense of direction which will be required when trying to look into some of the vulnerabilities that are present in the network or target's server.

The passive pilot study does not involve physically interacting with the target and that means that the IP address of the attacker is not logged. For instance, the attacker may search for the IP address of the target. It may be difficult to gain access to such information; however, it is also possible. The target will also not be able to notice that an attacker is trying to harvest some information as they plan an attack.

The passive reconnaissance will focus more on the business activities as well as the employees within the organization. The information that is readily available on the internet is known as OSINT (Open source Intelligence).

As for the passive reconnaissance, the attacker will interact with the target in a manner that is expected. For instance, the attacker will visit the website of the attacker. They will then view the available pages and they will then download some of the available documents. Some of these interactions are always expected and they are not detected easily and the target may not know that there is a looming attack.

The active reconnaissance involves interacting through port scanning in the specific network as well as sending direct queries that will then trigger the system alarms and that means that the target can easily capture the IP address of the attacker and their activities. The information that the target has gained can also be used to arrest the attacker. Additionally, the information can also be presented before a court of law as evidence that the attacker was planning something malicious. As for the active pilot study, there are various activities that the attacker should consider so that they can conceal their identity.

As an attacker, you should also follow some steps during the process of gathering information. The main focus is on the user account data. For the pilot study to be effective, as an attacker, you should always know what you are looking for. Also, make sure that you have gathered all the data that you need. Although the passive reconnaissance is less risky, it minimizes the amount of data that you can collect.

OSINT (Open-Source Intelligence)

This is the first step when planning an attack. In this case, the attacker should make use of the present search engines preferably Google. There is a lot of information that could come in handy when facilitating an attack. The process of collecting the information is quite complex.

In this book, we will just issue an overview since the main focus is on how to hack with Kali Linux. The essential highlights will offer some suitable guidance.

The information collected by an attacker will always depend on their initial motives and their major goals when they plan an attack. For instance, the attacker may want to access the financial data within a specific organization. Other types of information that they may need is the names of the employees. Most of the attackers will focus more on the senior employees who are working as executives. Some of these employees include the CFO among other seniors. The attacker will focus on obtaining their usernames and their respective passwords. In some instances, an attacker may try to carry out social engineering. In this case, they will have to supplement the information that they possess so that they may appear as credible individuals. After that, they can easily request for the information that they need.

As for the Open source Intelligence, the attacker will start by reviewing the online presence of the target. They will start by observing their social media pages, blogs, and websites. The public financial records also come in handy in some cases. The most important information is:

- The geographical location of the offices. For instance, there can be some satellite offices that also share some corporate information but they have not set up any measures that will ensure that the information is safe as it is being transmitted from one office to another.

- The overview of the parent and subsidiary firms matters especially when dealing with a new company that has also been acquired through M&A transactions. The acquired companies will not be as safe as compared to the parent company.

- The contact information and the names of the employees. The phone numbers and email addresses should also be obtained.

- Looking for clues about the target company's corporate culture so that it may be possible to facilitate the social engineering attack.

- The business partners are also eligible to access to network of the target.

- The technology being used. For instance, the target may issue a press release about how to adopt software and the attacker will go ahead and review the website of the vendor as they try to look for bug reports. After finding some vulnerabilities, they will be able to launch an attack.

Some of the online information sources that can also be used by an attacker when they are planning an attack include:

- Search engines including Google. There are also other search engines such as Bing. It's only that we have gotten used to Google. During the search process, you will realize that the process is highly manual. You may have to type the name of the company as well as other relevant details. Since technology has also advanced, there are some APIs that can be used to automate the searches of the search engines. Some of the effective APIs include Maltego.

There are other sources and they include:

- The financial and government sites since they provide some information about the key individuals within the company as well as some supporting data.

- The Usenet newsgroups. The man focus should be on the posts by the employees that you are targeting as a tester or an attacker. You may also seek some help with different forms of technology.

- Jigsaw and LinkedIn; these companies come in handy since they provide some information about the employees within a company.

- The cached content. It can be retrieved easily by search engines including Google.

- The country as well as the specific language being used.

- Employee and corporate blogs.

- Social media platforms such as Facebook.

- The sites whereby you can look up the server information and the DNS as well as routes. Some of these sites include myIPneighbors.com.

The main issue arises when you have to manage the information that you have found. The main advantage is that kali Linux has an application known as Keep Note.

It supports the rapid importation and management of different data types.

Route Mapping DNS reconnaissance

As a tester or an attacker, you will have to make sure that you have identified the targets that have an online presence. Make sure that you have also gained access to some of the items that may pose some interest. You will then go ahead and identify the IP addresses of the targets. The DNS reconnaissance will come in handy when identifying the domains as well as the DNS information that will help to define some of the IP addresses as well as actual domain names. The route between the attacker and the target will also be identified.

The information is easily available in some of the open sources. Some information is mainly present in some of the DNS registrars and they are referred to as third parties. The registrar may collect an IP address as well as some of the data requests that have been brought forth by an attacker. Such information is rarely provided to the specific target who will be a victim of an attack.

As for the target, they can easily monitor the DNS server logs. The information needed can also be obtained using an approach that is systematic.

WHOIS

The first step entails researching the IP address so as to identify the addresses that have also been assigned to the sites of the target. You will then make use of the whois command and it will allow you to query the databases that have also stored the information about certain users. The information that you will obtain includes the IP address and domain name.

The whois request will then come in handyu when providing physical addresses, names, e-mail addresses, as well as phone numbers. Such information is very important when it comes to performing a social engineering attack.

As an attacker or tester, you can use the whois command to carry out the following activities:

Supporting a social engineering attack against a target that has been identified using the whois query.

Identifying the location whereby you can launch a
   physical attack.

Conducting some research that will allow you to learn
more about the domain names that are present on the
server. You can also learn more about the number of
users operating it. As an attacker, you will also gain an
interest in learning whether the domains are insecure
and whether you can exploit the present vulnerabilities
to gain access while also compromising the target
server.

Identifying the phone numbers since you may also have
   to launch a dialing attack while conducting the social
   engineering attack.

The attack will then use the DNS servers to carry out
the DNS reconnaissance.

In some cases, the domain may be due to expire and
   the attacker may go ahead and try to seize the
   domain while also creating look-a-like website that
   will be used to lure unsuspecting visitors who think
   that they are entering into the original website.

To make sure that the data has been shielded
accordingly, there has been an increase in the use of

third parties. Also, when using public domains, you cannot access domains such as .gov and .mil. The mentioned domains belong to the military and the government and that is why they have been secured so that they cannot be accessed by other parties. When you send a request to such a domain, it will be logged. There are many online lists that can also be used to describe the IP addresses as well as domains. If you want to use the whois query, the following screenshot will offer some guidance when running the query against some of the Digital Defense domains:

There is a whois command record that will be returned and it will contain some names and geographical information as well as contact information that will come in handy when facilitating a social engineering attack. There are also many websites that are also used to automate the whois lookup. Some of the attackers use some of these sites to insert a step that will be between them and the attackers. The site that is doing the lookup may then log the IP address of the requester.

Mapping the Route to the Target

The route mapping was once used as a diagnostic tool. The tool would allow the attacker to view the route that is followed by the IP packet as it moves from one host to another. When using the TTL (time to live) field in the IP packer, an ICMP TIME_EXCEEDED message will then be elicited from one point to another. The message will be sent from the receiving router and it will also help to determine the value that is in the TTL field. The packets will also count the number of routes and hops that have been taken.

From the perspective of the attacker or penetration tester, the traceroute data will help to yield the following pieces of data:

The hints about the topology of the network.

The path that is present between the target and the attacker.

Identifying the firewalls and other devices that are used to control access to the network.

Identifying whether the network has been misconfigured.

In Kali Linux, you can map the route using the tracerouteis command. If you are using Windows, you can use the tracert command. If you happen to launch an attack when using Kali Linux, you will notice that most of the hops have been filtered. For instance, when using Google to trace the location of a certain target, the results will be as shown below:

If you were to run the same request when using the tracert on the Windows platform, you will see the following:

We will get the complete path and we have also noticed that Google is showcasing an IP address that is slightly different. The load balancers have also been indicated. The main reason why the path data is different is because the traceroute used the UDP datagrams whereas the Windows tracert will use the ICMP request (specifically the ICMP type 8). When you complete the traceroute when using the tools that have been provided by Kali Linux, you should also make sure that you have used multiple protocols so that you may obtain the complete path while also bypassing some of the devices that carry out packet-filtering.

Obtaining User Information

When an attacker or a penetration tester manages to gather the usernames and the e-mail addresses of the targets, they can then manage to gather into the systems. The most common tool that is deployed is the web browser and you have to perform a manual search. You have to search some of the third-party sites including Jigsaw and LinkedIn. You can also use some of the tools provided by Kali Linux to automate the search.

6. Your First Hack

As for the first hack, we can use a simple example detailing how to hack the WPA2 Wi-Fi networks using Kali Linux. Using such an example, the reader can get an overview of how to hack different systems before they try to hack into other systems that may be more complex.

Hacking the WPA2 Wi-Fi using Kali Linux

After learning about how to hack using Kali Linux as well as the tools that you may need to facilitate the attack, it is good to provide an example of how you can actually hack wireless networks. In this case, the example will entail hacking the WPA2 Wi-Fi network using Kali Linux.

When hacking a WPA2 network, make sure that you are conversant with some of the tools that Kali Linux has to offer. The operating system has some pre-installed tools and they are about 600 in total. You can also go ahead and install some other tools from the Kali Linux and GitHub repositories. Before installing other applications, you should ensure that each of the applications is verified. If you want to hack the WPA2 Wi-Fi, first make sure that you are conversant with various tools including the Aircrack-ng tool. There are some people who have been propagating rumors that it is possible to hack a WPA2 network using other operating systems such as Microsoft Windows. Such rumors are far-fetched and you should also note that only Kali Linux has the necessary tools that you can use to launch an attack on the WPA2 networks.

If you want to crack the network, make sure that you have installed the Kali Linux on your PC. If you want to successfully launch an attack on the WPA2 networks, ensure that you are conversant with the authentication processes of the WPA2 networks. Also, ensure that you also know your way around the Kali Linux operating system. If you are knowledgeable about how to launch such an attack, we will now discuss more about the steps that are involved when hacking into a WPA2 network successfully.

To successfully launch the attack, you need the following:

- Make sure that you have installed Kali Linux into your PC.

- Ensure you have a wireless adapter and it should also have capabilities such as monitor mode. There are some PCs that also have network cards and they are preferred in such a case. If the PC you are using does not have the network card, make sure that you have purchased it.
- Come up with a wordlist since it will be used when cracking the WPA2 network.
- You must be patient and spare enough time to handle the process.

After ensuring that you have heeded to all the requirements that have been outlined, you can follow these steps and you will be able to hack into the WPA2 network successfully.

The tutorial may come in handy; nevertheless, you should not hack into WPA2 networks without the necessary authorization. The tutorial will come in handy for the professionals who carry out security audits and penetration tests. After carrying out some tests, the ethical hackers are able to issue a detailed report indicating whether the network is safe or not. If there are some loopholes, some recommendations will be issued.

Step One:

Powering the computer and logging into Kali Linux.

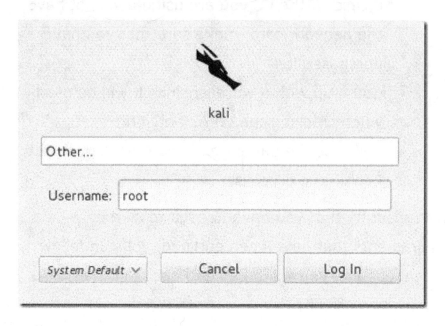

Step Two:

Ensure that you have plugged in the wireless adapter. When you run Kali Linux in the "Live Mode," ensure that you have also plugged in the wireless adapter and there is an icon that will also appear on the device menu and it is as shown below:

Step Three

Make sure that you are not connected to any wireless network. Also, open a terminal where you will key in the airmon-ng command.

```
root@kali:~# airmon-ng

Interface        Chipset         Driver

wlan0            Realtek RTL8187L        rtl8187 - [phy0]
```

The airmon-ng command lists all the wireless cards that will support the monitor mode. In an instance whereby there are no cards, make sure that you reconnected the network adapter and also inquire whether the monitor mode is supported by the card.

Step Four:

Open the terminal window and type the airmon-ng start command. After that, type the interface name of your wireless card. In this case, the interface name for our wireless card is wlan0; as a result, our command should be airmon-ng start wlan0.

```
root@kali:~# airmon-ng start wlan0


Found 2 processes that could cause trouble.
If airodump-ng, aireplay-ng or airtun-ng stops working after
a short period of time, you may want to kill (some of) them!
-e
PID      Name
3115     NetworkManager
3464     wpa_supplicant


Interface        Chipset          Driver

wlan0            Realtek RTL8187L          rtl8187 - [phy0]
                              (monitor mode enabled on mon0)
```

As per the screenshot above, the monitor mode has also been enabled. The new interface has been named mon0.

Step Five:

Key in the airodump-ng command in the monitor interface. A new monitor interface will be added and it is named mon0.

```
root@kali:~# airodump-ng mon0
```

Step Six:

The airodump command ensures that you can gain access to a list that contains all the wireless networks within your locality. You can also gain access to important information about the networks that have been listed. First, ensure that you have located the network that you will crack. After identifying one network that you are interested in, you should click Ctrl + C and the entire process will stop. Ensure that you have noted the channel of the network target.

Step Seven:

Copy the BSSID of the target network.

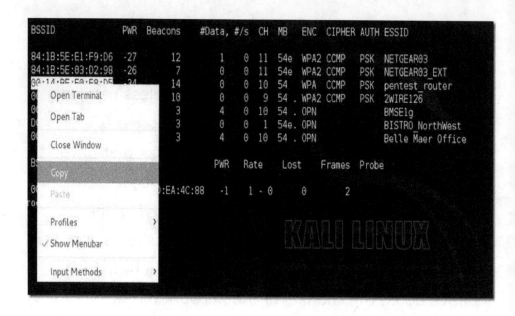

BSSID	PWR	Beacons	#Data, #/s	CH	MB	ENC	CIPHER	AUTH	ESSID
84:1B:5E:E1:F9:D6	-27	12	1	0	11	54e	WPA2	CCMP	PSK	NETGEAR03
84:1B:5E:03:D2:98	-26	7	0	0	11	54e	WPA2	CCMP	PSK	NETGEAR03_EXT
00:14:D5:E0:E0:D5	-34	14	0	0	10	54	WPA	CCMP	PSK	pentest_router

Open Terminal ... 10 0 0 9 54 . WPA2 CCMP PSK 2WIRE126

Open Tab ... 3 4 0 10 54 . OPN BMSE1g

3 0 0 1 54e. OPN BISTRO_NorthWest

Close Window ... 3 4 0 10 54 . OPN Belle Maer Office

Copy

			PWR	Rate	Lost	Frames	Probe

Paste ... :EA:4C:88 -1 1 - 0 0 2

Profiles >

✓ Show Menubar

Input Methods >

KALI LINUX

Open the terminal window and key in this command-
airodump-ng -c [channel] --bssid [bssid] -w
/root/Desktop/ [monitor interface]
Ensure that you have replaced the target's channel with
yours in the network. Go ahead and copy-paste the
BSSID of the target network and replace the name of
the monitor interface with mon0 since it is the name of
your monitor interface. The "-w" and the file path will
go ahead and specify where the intercepted handshakes
will be saved by the airodump so that you can hack the
Wi-Fi network at ease. In this instance, the handshakes
will be saved on the desktop.

The entire command is as shown below:

airodump-ng -c 10 --bssid 00:14:BF:E0:E8:D5 -w
/root/Desktop/ mon0

```
airodump-ng -c 10 --bssid 00:14:BF:E0:E8:D5 -w /root/Desktop/ mon0
```

Press enter to launch the command.

Step Eight:

Use the airodump command so that you can monitor the network. The command will also allow you to capture specific pieces of information about the target network. In this instance, we have to wait for the device to connect to the network. The router usually sends four-way handshakes and the attacker can capture them and they will eventually crack the Wi-Fi password. Four files will also be present on the desktop. The handshake is present in one of the folders on the desktop and you should make sure that none of the desktop folders is deleted.

Some people are usually impatient and it means that they may not be willing to wait for the device to connect. If you do not want to wait, you should use one of the tools belonging to the Aircrack suite. Some of the tools that you can use include the aireplay-ng; the tool comes in handy if you want to speed up the entire process. The tool ensures that the device has reconnected; first, some deauthentication packets are usually sent and they will trigger the reconnection. The packets will ensure that the network device thinks that it must reconnect and that means that as an attacker, you will not have to wait for a prolonged period.

When using this tool, you must ensure that there is someone who is connected to the target network. Also, keep track of the airodump-ng tool while waiting for the specific client to show up. The process might take longer.

In the screenshot below, the client has already connected to the network and that means that the Wi-Fi hacking process can proceed.

Step Nine:

Ensure that the airodump-ng is running. The hacker should open another terminal window and key in this command:

If you are using the default mode, you will notice that there is a shortcut named -0. There will be a number 2 and it will be representing the number of packets that you can send by default. −Indicates the router's BSSID and it will also be replaced by 00:14:BF:E0:E8:D5. −c indicates the client's BSSID and it will be replaced eventually. The complete command is as shown below:

Step Ten:

When you press Enter, the aireplay-ng command will send the packets. If you are close enough to the target, you can facilitate the deauthentication process accordingly. Some messages will also appear on the airodump screen.

```
WPA handshake: 00:14:BF:E0:E8:D5
```

The screenshot above showcases that the handshake has been captured. After the password has been acquired, the aireplay-ng terminal should be closed. You should then click Ctrl + C and make sure that the airodump-ng is still running. The tools will stop and monitor the network. In an instance whereby you need more information, you should not close the terminal window.

There are various instances, you may not receive the "handshake message." It means that some issues were present when the packets were being sent. Some challenges may arise in the process. Ensure that you have moved closer. There are some devices that may also not be able to reconnect automatically and it means the deauthentication process may fail when you try to reconnect. Make sure that you have tried new devices or also leave the airodump running while waiting for someone to reconnect to the target network. There are some instances when you might be close to the network, and you should make use of the spoofing tools. Some of the widely used spoofing tools include Wi-Fi Honey. When using such a tool, the devices may be tricked into thinking that you are the router. To successfully launch the attack, make sure that you are very close to the target. If you are not close to the target, do not attempt to hack the network since your attempts will prove to be futile. You can use some of these tools to hack WPA2 networks. There are some networks that may also be cracked when you are using some of these tools. The networks that cannot be cracked easily are the ones that have long passwords that have many characters.

Step 11:

All the steps during the hacking process are external and this is the last process whereby the attacker cracks the WPA2 networks. There are four files situated in the desktop and they were generated during the retrieval of the handshake messages. The most important file, in this case, is the one with the .cap command. Open a new terminal and key in this command:

The Aircrack tool will then use the −a method. The tool comes in handy when you want to crack the handshake. There is a −b and it stands for the BSSID and it will also replace the BSSID of the router with the BSSID of the target of the router. The BSSID, in this case, is 00:14:BF:E0:E8:D5. There is a −w and it represents the wordlist. It shall be replaced with a path to the wordlist and you will have to download it. There is a wordlist located in the root folder and it is named "wpa.txt." The .cap file is located in the /root/Desktop/*cap. The password is also contained in that folder.

This is the complete command:

aircrack-ng −a2 −b 00:14:BF:E0:E8:D5 −w /root/wpa.txt /root/Desktop/*.cap

```
aircrack-ng -a2 -b 00:14:BF:E0:E8:D5 -w /root/wpa.txt /root/Desktop/*.cap
```

Press enter.

Step 12:

Launch the Aircrack-ng will also be launched and it will crack the password used to access the WPA2 network. You can only crack the password if it is present in the wordlist that you had compiled. There are instances whereby you may be unable to crack the network if the exact password is not present in the wordlist. The wordlist comprises of numerous passwords that are supposedly used to access the WPA2 target network. After a failed attempt, compile a new wordlist. If you are unable to crack the network, that is an indicator that the network is safe from external attackers. Even when an attacker launches a brute-force attack, they cannot attack a WPA2 network that is secure. In some instances, the WPA2 hacking process may take longer. Make sure that you have considered the length if the wordlist. If the correct password is present in the wordlist, the Aircrack-ng should look like this:

```
Opening /root/Desktop/-01.cap
Reading packets, please wait...

                        Aircrack-ng 1.2 beta3


             [00:00:00] 192 keys tested (1409.45 k/s)


                      KEY FOUND! [ notsecure ]


     Master Key     : 42 28 5E 5A 73 33 90 E9 34 CC A6 C3 B1 CE 97 CA
                      06 10 96 05 CC 13 FC 53 B0 61 5C 19 45 9A CE 63

     Transient Key  : 86 D0 43 C9 AA 47 F8 03 2F 71 3F 53 D6 65 F3 F3
                      86 36 52 0F 48 1E 57 4A 10 F8 B6 A0 78 30 22 1E
                      4E 77 F0 5E 1F FC 73 69 CA 35 5B 54 4D B0 EC 1A
                      90 FE D0 B9 33 06 60 F9 33 4B CF 30 B4 A8 AE 3A

     EAPOL HMAC     : 8E 52 1B 51 E8 F2 7E ED 95 F4 CF D2 C6 D0 F0 68
root@kali:~#
```

In this case, the password to the network is "notsecure." You can note that the password is present in the wordlist that was used during the hacking process. In some instances, you can gain access to the password without struggling a lot. As the attacker, you can also change the password to the network and that way you can gauge whether the network is indeed secure. When you change the password, it will all work out to your advantage. After accessing the network, you will also be able to gain access to some sensitive pieces of information.

7. Ethical Hacking and Penetration Testing

There is a misconception among most people which is that they think ethical hacking and penetration testing is both the same thing. However, in reality, it is not so in actual. Not only normal human beings who are not acquainted with the world of cyber security but the cyber security experts also get confused at times between the two. Although both of them fall under the same section of offensive security, there is a thin line that differentiates both. Offensive security is composed of various objects such as penetration testing, reverse engineering of software, social engineering, ethical hacking and many more.

In the world of cyber security, both the items ethical hacking and penetration testing are of utter importance. Let's have a look at some of the aspects of both the components.

Penetration Testing

Penetration testing, as the name goes by, can be understood that it is a process of testing whether penetration is possible or not. It looks out for all sorts of vulnerabilities, risks, malicious content and flaws within a system. By system, it can either be a computer system or an online server or network. This process is done for the purpose of strengthening the system of security in an organization for the sole purpose of defending the infrastructure of IT. It is a procedure which is official in nature and can be regarded as very helpful and not at all a harmful attempt if used wisely. Penetration testing is an essential part of ethical hacking where it is focused on the attempt of penetrating a system of information.

As it is very helpful in readily improving the overall strategies of cyber security, the process of penetration testing needs to be performed at regular intervals. Several forms of malicious content are built up for finding out the weak points within an application, program or system. The malware is spread throughout the network for testing the vulnerabilities. Pentest might not be able to sort out all forms of concerns regarding security, but it can actually minimize the chances of any attack. Penetration testing helps in determining whether an organization or company is vulnerable to any form of cyber attack or not, whether the measures of defense are on point and which of the security measures needs to be changed for decreasing system vulnerability.

Penetration testing can easily show the strengths and weaknesses of the structure of an IT system at one point of time. The pentesting process is not at all a casual process. It comes with lots of planning, granting of permission for pentesting from the management and then starting the process without preventing the normal flow of work in an organization.

Ethical Hacking

The role of an ethical hacker is somewhat similar to that of a penetration tester. But, the process of ethical hacking comes with various forms of diversified duties. Ethical hacking encompasses all the methodologies of hacking along with all forms of methods related to cyber attack. The process of ethical hacking is targeted to the identification of vulnerabilities and also fixes all of them just before any attacker can exploit the information for the purpose of executing cyber attack. Ethical hacking is being called as ethical as all the required functions are performed only after the granting of required permissions from the authority for intruding the system of security. The ethical hackers perform their role on the ground of ethics whereas the attackers hack without any prior alarm.

The role of a professional ethical hacker is very critical as well as complex as the person who is intruding the system of security needs to perform everything without even affecting the overall functioning of the system and then locate the available vulnerabilities as well. The ethical hacker traces out the possible vulnerabilities and reports the authority about the required measures. An ethical hacker not only works with the methodologies of security but also suggests the implementation of the same. The safety of an IT infrastructure is in the hands of an ethical hacker.

Penetration testing Vs. Ethical hacking

Although the functioning of both penetration testing and ethical hacking might seem similar but both differ from each other in various aspects. The main goal of penetration testing is to look out for vulnerabilities within a specific environment. In the case of ethical hacking, it uses various types of attacks for finding out the flaws in security. Penetration testing deals with the security of a particular area whereas ethical hacking itself is a comprehensive term and pentesting is a function of the ethical hacker. For being a good pentester, past experience is required in the field of ethical hacking. Ethical hacking is one step towards pentesting. Unless and until someone knows the methodologies properly, they will not be able to carry on with a penetration testing.

Penetration testing does not require very detailed writing of reports. However, in the case of an ethical hacker, an ethical hacker needs to be an expert report writer. Paper work is comparatively less in penetration testing when compared to ethical hacking. In the case of ethical hacking, detailed paper work with legal agreements is required. Penetration testing consumes very less time which is not the case with ethical hacking. It requires a lot more time and effort. For penetration testing, accessibility of the overall system is not required. In the case of ethical hacking, a hacker requires complete accessibility of the target system.

Bottom line

As penetration testing techniques are being used for protecting the systems from all forms of threats, the attackers are also coping up with the same and are coming up with new vulnerability points in the target applications. So, it can be said that some sort of penetration testing is not at all sufficient for protecting the system of security. This is not the case with ethical hacking as it effectively finds out the loopholes and reports about the same for further improvement. There are many cases where it has been found that when a new vulnerability has been found in a system, the attackers hacked the system immediately after the testing. However, it does not imply that penetration testing is not useful at all. It cannot prevent an attack from taking place but can help in the improvement of a system.

8. Solving Level Problems

Since it is extremely simple, it is just meant to make you understand some of the concepts you will need to move on to the next levels. I will take this space to explain. Our main objective at level0, as in all others, is to get the password to the next level. This can be done by running the vo pass, which is in the bin directory. Try connecting to HackersLab and typing pass. A screen appears that will wax and show you the level0 password. So, to get the password for thelevel1, do I have to login as this user? How is this possible?

There is another way. At every level, there is a file that has the UID (user identification number) higher than yours and the GID (Identical group identification number). The task is: how to explore this file so that through it you can execute the pass command and get the next password? Now if we do this through it and it has a higher user privilege (UID), our system will "think" that we are the other user. Difficult? Let's see an example.

Suppose we connect to HackersLab. Let's create one imaginary level0, just as a test: 8 Login: level08

Password: [level0 @ level0] $ whoamilevel0 [level0 @ level0] $ idUID = 2000 GID = 2000 OTHER ANY = 9999 So far, what have we achieved? We have successfully logged in to level0, we have entered the whoami command, which informed us that the username is level0, and the id command, which provided us with user IDs (UID), group IDs (GID), and other things that will not be needed for us.

Now I will have the system search for files that have a UIDsuperior to ours. For example, if our UID is 2000, then I want to search for files that have UID 2001 (level1). [level0 @ level0] $ find / -uid 2001 –gid 2000/ tmp / suzuki: Permission Denied/ bin / joy: Permission Denied/ etc / test/ usr / local / yu: Permission Denied/ var / shenmue: Permission Denied.

I asked the system to show me all the files that they allowed and are user level1 (which has UID 2001) and group level0 (from GID 2000). Why look for the GID? Simple. The file needs to be from our group so that we can manipulate it. This will become clearer in a moment. We only found the / etc / test file. Everything else with Permission Denied is rubbish.

How to list, then, only the files we want? [level0 @ level0] $ find / -uid 2001 −gid 2000 2> / dev / null/ etc / test Redoing the command, I included the string 2> / dev / null , which I told the system" anything not necessary (2) send to (>) the trash (/ dev / null)". Thus, we only got the result we expected. So, let's list the in-file formations. [level0 @ level0] $ ls −la / etc / test-rwx — x— 1 level1 level0 10876 Mar 8 06:24 test.

From the information, we confirmed what we wanted. It is a file created by user level1 and that belongs to group level0. The user who created it has the permission of total users, group users are allowed to execute only, and others not even that. Just out of curiosity, I could browse the file using the username instead of UID? Of course!

Let's check: Let's try the id command. Oh! A surprise! A new ID has appeared with EUID number 2001 (level1). This EUID didn't exist before ... it was given to us by the program. We will then try the whoami command, just to take the doubts. That!! The command informed us that we are level1 (or at least that we have permission from level1). How could .hi do this? Simple, he was a backdoor.funds or trojan horse). The moment we ran it, he ran the/ bin / sh command and created another shell (command session) within the first one, but with your permissions. This means that if we try to type thepass command (which returns the level password), now we get ...The password for the next level !!! The password for level1, then, is the newworld.

Level 1 Problem

Login: level18 Password: newworld Study: External Execution of Commands and Pipes.

The necessary knowledge to have at this level is to know how to take advantage of a program that executes external commands. If the program has an EUID (ID) higher than yours, this can be a serious issue. For a demonstration, let's follow the example of level0. I will create an imaginary level1, with dummy files, as a test. Login: level18 Password: [level1 @ level1] $ find / -user level2 -group level1 2> /dev / null/ usr / bin / list[level1 @ level1] $ cd / usr / bin[level1 @ level1 bin] $ ./ listEnter a file: / usr / bin / list-rwx — x— level2 level1 876 Jun 23 13:12 / usr / bin / list.

Let's take a slow look at what we did. We are supposed to log in to the HackersLab system, we look for the file (s) that have level2 UID and Level1 GID (if you still don't understand why the search is done this way, re-read level0). We found the file / usr / bin / list .I tried to run it and got it. He asked me for any file and informed me the same as we were using, just to see what would happen (could be any other). The list program then returned me information about the file I provided. The problem is there. The list executed from within it the command is -lato show file information. He performed the following on the system: [level1 @ level1] $ ls -la / usr / bin / list-rwx — x— level2 level1 876 Jun 23 13:12 / usr / bin / list But he executes with privileges superior to ours (forgot that your creative user and IDs are level2???). So what can we do to add another command since it executes ls externally? The easier way is using the pipe (|), which we saw in the command section. He will allow you to enter another command to be executed. But where will we do it? Let's run the list again: level1 @ level1 bin] $ ./ list. Enter a file: / usr / bin / list Here is the secret. Instead of just putting the PATH of the file, how about we add the pipe and some command in front? Would be like this: Enter a file: / usr / bin / list | pass That! If our theory is right, it will run ls, listing ourprogram / usr / bin / list and then immediately run the program in the for-provides the passwords. Complete now: level1 @ level1 bin] $ ./ list. Enter a file: / usr / bin / list | pass-rwx — x— level2 level1 876 Jun 23 13:12 / usr / bin / list The password for level2 is ...Ready! We get a new password. Let's get to the real walkthrough now.

Step by step Log in to HackersLab and log in with the level1 password. The first thing to do (already classic) is type the command find / -userlevel2 -group level1 2> / dev / null to find our target file. We found two, / proc / 20840 and / usr / bin / amos . But wait a minute ... Amos is the name of a prophet (dim, dim, dim ... we found why this tip level). Let's check the amos file, then: Seeing the information from the masters, we find that again we have group permission to execute it (x). We managed to rotate it without needing " ./ " (slash) before it means that it is in the PATH. How did it happen in our study session simulation? The program asks us the PATH of any file. We put the file we are currently running (such as said before, can be anyone). He informed us that it is executable.

Getting back to the problem at this level, we saw that Matthew had to use the file command to make the amos program. So, is the program running externally file archives? You? Let's try it out! Yes!! The sample runs the file externally. Let's try to run it and make a pipe to try to get your privilege. So let's do it the same way we study: we put the information for / usr / bin / amos, the | (pipe) and the pass command. Thus, the program will have the file / usr /bin / mas | pass. Result? The password for level2. One more stage won.

Level 2 Problem

Kevin, a BBS programmer, wants to add an alert on your homepage so your members can see your posts every time they log in. Unfortunately, the message has more than one page and its members cannot read it. As a result, he has been warming his brain night and day, trying to find a solution. Finally, he considered using the more command to solve your problem. However, this method is risky because of security issues. TIP: Nuff said!

Login: level28 Password: DoItYourself Study: Shells and Subshells

The shell of a system is nothing but the execution of a shell interpreter commands entered. It is a text-mode screen in which you can interact through system commands. In the DOS system, for example, the command interpreter is the command.com file. At the Windows NT and compatible, it is cmd.exe. You can prove it on NT by going to Start / Run and typing cmd. A command screen will open.

Level 3 Problem

Login: level38 Password: hackerproof Study: PATH and IFS HackersLab

Levels 3 and 4 are pretty much the same, in the two; you will need to understand the concept of PATH, IFS, and export. These levels at the beginning of the challenge are really interesting and difficult ones (you will see later level5 and 6 are much easier). Although the book focuses on how to break a Linux system, I will explain the PATH in brief. Learning this term makes it easier to understand others. First, let's go to the concept:

PATH is the absolute path of directories, where the system always looks for a file to run. For example, typing in the root of a system the commands ls, dir, date or any other, the OS will search directoriesPATH by these commands and execute them. If not, it will return an error. Complicated? Not so much.

Let's look at a simple example. In the above DOS example, I listed the data that was in the directory called test director. I found that there was a program called app.exe. I then tried to run the app from the root. I received an error saying that the command is not recognized (not found). So, I modified the PATH and pointed it to the test director where was the app. Just use PATH = C: \ directoriotest. I tried to run the app again and voila! It rolled right. Of course, now the command was inside the system search PATH. Okay, but how does this relate to a hacking challenge? All. Imagine that a Windows application externally calls the send NET.EXE (the command that controls the NetBIOS protocol, and may be connected to shares, sends messages, enables users, etc.). What would happen to this program if I had created another with the same name (NET.EXE), put it in the test director and set the PATH? NET would be run normally by the individual program, but my NET, which could be an intrusion program like a backdoor (or horsebackTrojan).

Going back to Linux, then imagine that Steven's program simply writes the date. That's easy, just create a fake version in a directory (whichever one you want to choose), move the PATH there and export it (send it back to the system).

But we have a problem ... What if his program runs directly / bin / date instead of just date? Even if we modified PATH, the program would be running directly in the directory ... Now what? Who can help us? The fearless IFS. The IFS or Internal Field Separator has an interesting feature – you can give it an ASCII character and whenever a command is typed in the system, this character will be separated. This process has some very interesting uses: In our problem, the Steven program runs directly / bin / date on the system. If we configure IFS as follows: export IFS = / (configuring and exporting to the system in only one line, saves time) What will this entail? Instead of the program running /bin/date, it will run bin date (as two separate commands) because IFS has removed the slash. Well, if it will run date, it will fall on our nasty PATH and we'll be able to break the system ...If you still have questions, they will be taken now in the practical part.

Repeating the (already starting to get boring) process of connecting to HackersLabas level3 and look for the file made by steven, we found the file today (which is curiously in the / usr / man / en / man8 / directory which is the Brazilian Portuguese version of the manual that comes with Linux). We listed the file (only usual) and we saw that it has permission to execute.

Enter the file directory and type the pwd command just to confirm (to show the current directory). Try rotating the file by typing ./today, this way, it returns me the date. Everything is now following what was specified in the initial problem.

Enter the date command as a test and it returns the results in the common format. This is not necessary to be done, it is just curiosity. Entering the set command (shows, changes, and creates system variables, we saw the PATH. The executable file date, which is used externally, is inside the bin directory. Let us then take the necessary steps – those explained in the study.

Level 4 Problem

Login: level4 Password: AreUReady? Study: More Deduction and More PATH.

Level 4 is very similar to the third. Everything I showed in that level study in the past applies here. But there is a big difference. How did I know that? According to the problem, Kevin added just one line of code in your game. This line of code could be anything ... a message on the screen, a comment, or an external command being executed. There is only one way you know: running the game and trying to identify some command it is running (Does it list directories? Show date? Time?). There are commands like strace and others you can use to try to figure out external references. But the easiest way is by trying to run the game and find out. The big difference I was referring to is this: at level3, you knew which should impersonate the date command, but at this level, besides you knowing which command is used, you are not sure if this is the right procedure. Only by analyzing it will you know. Let's go to step by step and check how the procedure should be.

We connect to HackersLab as level4 and look for files with a per-level5 user mission. We found our game, the trojan file, which is inside the / usr / games directory. Let's run it to see what happens. The game prompts you to select the speed with which you want to play. That game is a kind of Tetris. An interesting thing that we saw here is that the game cleared the screen when it started. And it also cleans the screen many times while you play. Is it then the clear command, which clears the screen, running externally? Let's follow this deduction and try to proceed as at level3.

Again, we export PATH to the / home / level4 / tmp directory (the only one we can record). We also exported IFS to the system. We have a file called clear inside our recording directory and we use the / bin / pass command inside it. If that's right then, when we run trojka, it would have the same effect as the past level, but now with the program executed, we have cleared the bad one. So...Silent night, holy night! And onwards to level5 !

Level 5 Problem

Login: level5 Password: Silent night, holy night! Study: Strings in Binaries.

First, what is a string? It's a char grouping, as taught in college. In common language, it is a word, a sentence or a text. Whenever we program, we need to use strings to communicate with each other and with the user. Two examples in different languages of strings for the user. Pascal writeln ('Enter a number'); 8 C ++ cout >> "Enter a number \ n"; Strings are also used to make simple comparisons of words and phrases.

I know all programmers are tired of seeing this, but a basic explanation is important for non-programmers not to get so lost. A comparison example: Test Program; varx : string; beginwriteln (' Enter your password: '); readln (x); if x = ' binladen ' then beginwriteln (' Correct Password '); endelse beginwriteln (' Incorrect password '); end; end;

In this little program in Pascal, I first send the user a text requesting your password. I read the variable that contains the password and then the comparison: if the string (password) is the same as binladen, I write in that the password is correct, otherwise, type Incorrect password. This is nothing new to anyone. Here, what is interesting to us will be the compiled program and not the source. When we do not use an encryption feature or executables in our compiled program, it leaves most of our strings on display. You can see this using a hexadecimal edit. But there is an easier way, the strings command, which scans any binary file (not just executables) and shows you the strings found. I will compile the code shown earlier in DOS and show the problem step by step. I did the program and tested it.

I typed saddamhussein as a password. It returned incorrect password, so I tested with the default password, binladen. The program returned the correct password. Soon after, I'll type the strings command progteste.exe to try and find the string binladen.

Oops ... Quickly, looking at the result generated by the strings command, we found four interesting lines: Type your password: bin Laden. Correct password and so we can figure out simple passwords without using neither the encryption features nor some compression on any executable. We saw it in DOS, but what about Linux? So, let's go step by step.

We connect to HackersLab as level5. We are looking for the target file, the new modified backdoor location cited in the problem. We found / lib / security /pam_auth.so (file pam_auth.so within the directory / lib / security). I listed your information and again we are allowed to execute. Let's do it then.

We ran pam_auth.so and he asked for the password, we put any string of words and it returned Password incorrect. Let's first check your directory for more interesting files. There are many files. We would waste a lot of time trying the command strings in each and every one. So, we will try the main one, pam_auth.so. Will we find something interesting? We found several possible passwords: abcd1234, loveyou!, flr1234 and we will have to try all of these ones by one as a level6 password. There are also two phrases that could be passwords: what the hell are you thinking? And Best of The Best Hackerslab. Hmmm, this Best of TheBest Hackerslab is very suspicious. Let's try it first.

Best of The Best Hackerslab was the correct password. Direct to the top level. If you want, instead of going straight to logging in as level6 and entering the password, use the right password on the backdoor to make John angry again!

Level 6 Problem

Login: level6 Password: Best of The Best Hackerslab Study: Port Scan.

This is one of the easiest levels of HackersLab. It's for a really relaxed time. It focuses on the following fact: there is a second open door for access to the system. What are these doors? Whenever you connect to a system, a "Socket" is created. A socket is nothing more than the IP + address combination service door. This allows the same internet address to have multiple services running as Web Server, FTP, SMTP, POP, and others.Some common port numbers:21 - FTP22 - SSH23 - TELNET25 - SMTP79 - FINGER80 - WWW3128 - PROXY6000 – XWINDOWSSERVER, common ports using TCP and UDP protocols.

For example: when I connect to any web page like http://www.visualbooks.com.br, I'm actually connecting to HTTP: //www.visualbooks.com.br:80 (visualbooks.com.br, on port 80, which is the web standard). So far it seems easy. But we fall into the following problem - there are 65535 ports for both TCP and UDP protocols. There are doors that never end anymore. How can we find out which ones are open and which aren't? By using door scanners. Port scanners are applications that try to find out in a certain IP address or host, which ports are open. They can usually use a list of most known ports, or a range (example: from 1000 to 8000). They are usually extremely fast and results quickly return to us. Common port scanners perform a TCP connect () on the most targeted machine. This means that it performs the three TCP authentication paths (syn- syn / ack-ack). Using this system, it is easy for the scanner to discover the scanning attempt. A firewall or IDS, for example, quickly captures the hacker's IP. To end this, there are now more sophisticated scanners, like NMAP.NMAP, which can scan in many ways besides TCP connect (), has half syn () scanning (only sent syn), fin, Xmas and others. Each type uses different flags to make it difficult to detect the scanned host. At this step-by-step level, I will use two different scanners: NMAP, for Linux, and VALHALLA for Windows and we'll try to find the port.

Level 7 Problem

Login: level7 Password: Can't help falling in love Study: Breaking Unix / Linux Passwords.

Many older hackers are already used to the words DES, shadow, Cracker Jack, John the Ripper ... shame the new generation doesn't have such intimacy with these terms. Unix / Linux uses a password encryption system called DES. This system creates an encrypted string and places it in the security file.system names which are usually / etc / passwd. Used to use now / etc /shadow. They moved to the shadow archive hoping to increase the security, leaving the original password with only the usernames. Those who take control of the system can get any file, even the shadow. A typical shadow entry: mflavio: yFdrXa1EwNYng: 12126: 0: 99999: 7 ::: According to the previous information, we have the username asmflavio. Encrypted Password: yFdrXa1EwNYng. The rest of the numbers are System IDs (UID, GID, etc.).

Great, I have a user's password on Linux, but it's encrypted! No problem, I'll get a program that decrypts. That sounds feasible, but that's impossible. As I said before, DES creates a hash, which is a one-way encryption system. It cannot be decrypted. But then ... how do we find out the password? Just use your imagination. Think: if the password in shadow cannot be decrypted, how does the system compare this password with the password that the user types when logging in? Easy. The system encrypts the new password and compares the two encrypted values. If they are equal, that is the password CrackerJack and John The Ripper are programs that allow you to use a wordlist or brute force to "crack" Unix /Linux. They will encrypt each word using DES and compare it with the password that is in the password file. If the result hits ... that's the right password. Of course, for this, you need to have a good wordlist. A wordlist contains passwords commonly used and divided into categories like movie names, German words, etc ...Let's see again, in practice, how this process is done.

We log into HackersLab and look for the file with UID level8 and GIDlevel7. We found / dev / audio2 . We enter the / dev directory and run ./audio. The program shows some trash on the screen. But is it really rubbish? It shows three strings (which could probably also be obtained using this string) command: level8, shadow, and VoE4HoQCFfMW2. Well, I deduced a little bit, by the hash face of the last string and the other two, I think we found the password ... encrypted.

We will have to try to find out the password using John the Ripper (which can be obtained at http://www.blackcode.com). But first, we need to stop the wordlist and adapt the encrypted password. Is there a way you can try to figure out the password just by typing the hash as John the Ripper's command line? For this, you could use a single option. But for study questions, we took a shadow file and replaced the root password with our obtained hash. Thus, we simulated and cracked a shadow file. The JTR (John The Ripper) will try all the words in this list as passwords. The list has been saved as passwords.txt. Now, let's use JTR. JTR was executed as john –wordfile: passwords.txt shadow (sig-Nice: Dear John, please use the wordlist passwords.txt to remove passwords which will be tested in shadow). It quickly returned the password to me.

It is wonderfu. What a strange word is that? Pen-a little while later we find out: wonderfu actually is wonderful only from English), one of the words on our list. But why did he only show eight characters (the last one is the missing "l")? This is the same problem that occurs when the Program File directory becomes a file. The program is DOS-based, and it can show only eight characters. Of course, you can change that in the rules. To learn more, take a look at the JTR manual. What matters is that the password for level8 is wonderful!

Level 8 Problem

Login: level8 Password: wonderful Study: Race Conditions.

At this point, a lot of changes in the HackersLab challenge. Levels below these were pretty simple so there wasn't much to talk about studying, this change now from race conditions. They are conceived a little more complicated than we dealt with till now and these require a greater knowledge (including code examples) to be properly understood. If you don't know C, it would be better if you had a notion before, but for now, it doesn't matter. Understanding the general concept behind the problem is already a step forward.

This much theoretical introduction of the race condition problem is necessary to understand how it occurs, how problems occur between two reads and write functions and get a sense of which functions can be used to correct a certain problem. If you have no notion of C and were "floating" in the explanation, I suggest you try to learn a little, because all levels after this will use programming. This level was much higher than the previous ones and it will be easy to understand step by step.

We connect to HackersLab as level8, we find the file for level9 UID and level8 GID. We found what was mentioned in the problem, /usr / bin /ps2. After entering the / usr / bin directory , I tried to run ./ps2 . Nothing happens ... but really? We know that it creates a temporary file, but suppose that we were not told about it. So we can "check" our actions using the strace command. Typing strace / usr / bin / ps2 (without the quotation marks). Let's take a look at what the command generated: Sounds like a joke ... there is everything we saw in the study ... the open () function opening a temporary file without any descriptor checks, attempting to write the string hahahahahahaha using the write () function without reading any of the permissions, and worse, giving us the filename instead of creating a random file.

Let's try to create some "little scripts" to link the temporary file /var/tmp2/ps2.tmp created by the ps2 program to some content of our interest. You will have to use the VI text editor to create two small little programs or scripts. One will be running the ps2 file so we can enjoy our race condition before it "closes" the /var/tmp2/ps2.tmp file. Just type vi <file name> . In the first script, for example, create a file named race1 (or other filename) inside the var / directorytmp2 (or other temporary directory) using the vi / var / tmp2 / race1 command. The same goes for the second script. When starting the VI, type " a " to enter edit mode and press Esc to return to program mode. race1 while trueof/ usr / bin / ps2donerace2while trueof/ usr / bin / ps2 &rm -rf /var/tmp2/ps2.tmpln -sf / var / tmp2 / race1 /var/tmp2/ps2.tmpdone. A little tip about VI: When you're done typing, press the Esc key; to save (after pressing Esc), type: w (colon+ w); and to exit: q (colon + q), as in the following example: Let's take a look. Both scripts will loop. The first (race1) normally runs the ps2 file but keeps repeating, giving us a long time to change the temporary file. Already the second script (race2), runs the ps2 program again, but as background (using do &), thus giving us even more time to win the race. In the loop, race2 tries to remove the temporary file and replace it with a link to the race1 file.

Let's go line by line to not complicate: / usr / bin / ps2 & (run the program again);rm -rf /var/tmp2/ps2.tmp (delete temporary file);ln -sf / var / tmp2 / race1 /var/tmp2/ps2.tmp (overrides the temp- a link to the first script, so the program will try to record the string in our script instead of the temporary file). Having created both scripts, we will have to give them execute permission. IS just type the commands: chmod + x race1 and chmod + x race2, as shown in the permissions before chmod and after? Now we can execute. Now we have to do something unheard of in HackersLab: We connect it twice. That is, you will have to open two telnet windows and log in as level8 twice at the same time. In one of the windows, you will rotate race1 by typing ./race1, and in the other, race2 by typing ./race2. You will get some "junk" on the screen when you run both, something like "existing file".

But after running race2, if race1 is already running, your "trash" will become this:

"Congratulations!!! Your race attack was a success ... the level9 password is! Secu! "

Note: At this level, there was no need to worry about/bin/pass file, since ps2 itself contained the password.

Level 9 Problem

Login: level9 Password:! Secu! Study: Overflow Buffers

We are looking for a file that has level10 UID and level9 GID. We found the file / etc / bof (what a suggestive name ... bof = bufferoverflow). We list your permissions and see something interesting. Besides our permission to execute, there is a bit there. It is a level10 SUID bit. Continuing to check, we ran the program. He asks you to put a nickname (nick_name). I wrote my name and he showed us on the screen "hello~ macros_flavio ". Just as a test, what would happen if I put a string too long? Would the program do "bound checking"? Or will I flood the buffer? Just testing to know ...I put a lot of "x" on the screen. An error occurred: Segmentation fault. Bingo!

Level 10 Problem

Until we finish the connection, We will have to keep spoofing and sniffing at the Target, really thinking that is talking to the victim. Of course, doing it "by hand" is horrible, so there are various applications to accomplish the process. We have dozens of them for Linux, like spoofit, lcrzoex (which is multiplatform) and others. We also have programs for Windows 2000 that spoof IP and MAC addresses. One is sterm, where it is super easy to configure IP spoofing, as shown in the following figure. Look at Appendix B where to get these programs. UDP Spoof Now that we've seen how spoofing is done on IP, it's easy to understand how we'll do a UDP spoof to get the next level HackersLab password. The principle is the same but much easier. UDP, unlike TCP, has no three-way authentication. It is considered an "unreliable" communication protocol because if a packet is lost it doesn't matter. UDP is widely used for broadcasting (when streaming some video or music on the Internet, for example). Consequently, we need not have to try to find out some type of sequence number to send a spoofed UDP packet to. Just get the header of this package (still on the root machine that allows usRAW packets) and include the new "spoofed" address. We have two options to do this: use the excellent hping tool(www.hping.org), which performs various types of spoofing, including UDP, with the exception of result lenses. Or we will write our own code in C to do so. As per a didactic question, we will have the second option.

Exchange my code email for yours, and you will receive the password. Remember in the beginning I said that few people can get through even at this level? Well, the problem is this: too many firewalls and routers block spoofed packets. That means there is a very good chance great that on the route between your computer and HackersLab, a router "Prevent" the spoiled package. How to do then? Try multiple routes ... I tried to run the program several free shells I could get on the Internet until from a shell of a friend of mine from Fortaleza worked and I received the password by email. Let's run it step by step to see then. Step by step So let's try our spoofing. In the figure below, we compile the udpspoofbr (or whatever name you want), which we saw the code in the sectionstudy, and we perform. He asked us for source IP, source port, destination IP and destination port. In the problem, it asked us to send a message as if it were from www.hackerslab.org, from any door, todrill.hackerslab.org on port 5555. So I typed the command like this: ./udpspoofbr www.hackerslab.org 1234 drill.hackerslab.org5555 Note that the source port makes no difference, so much so that we put1234. But I got a "socket failed" error. Of course, I have to be root to do it, or the system won't allow you to manipulate RAW packets to spoof. Let's try again as root.

Level 11 Problem

Just as stack overflow is a danger, so is heap overflow. Whenever we use the dangerous combination of non-limiting functions' buffer size with programs that have SUID bit and file rights .root, we created a big problem. Understanding this concept well, the walkthrough will be quite simple. Find the problem files, choose the exploit and change the values PROGVULN and ARQVULN. Step by step We connected to HackersLab and found the file / usr / local /bin/hof, quoted in the problem description. Let's take a look and see if it really causes a segmentation error. Let's execute it.

And there it is. He asked us for the level 11 password, and shortly thereafter a failed segmentation fault has occurred. It's our gateway, as in the stack. Only now there's a different thing. The program acts as follows: If we provide the correct password, it will access the passwd.success file (or access if the error did not occur), and if we make a mistake, it accesses passwd.fail. We will try to exploit passwd.success, using the segmentation error to access the contents of this file with the hof program's SUID permissions. I do our exploit in VI and set the PROGVULN constants to /usr /

local / bin / hof and ARQVULN as /usr/local/bin /
passwd.success. SavedWe compiled it (cc exploit.c -o
exploit) and that's it! Let's test and perform a little
brute force with hexadecimal addresses until we can.

Ready! After a few attempts with different addresses,
(note something: to find the right address, we were
trying to address until PATH / usr / local /bin/hof
appears full on the screen.). And voila! I want to love
forever is the password for level 13.

Level 12 Problem

Login: level128 Password: I want to love forever Study:
Simple Encryption

We have already discussed encryption, and from that
level, HackersLab started repeat techniques already
seen (read on other levels). At level 7, I had said we
must use the John the Ripper program to try to find out
the password encrypted.

Of course, the chances are slim when encryption
involves Lots of numbers. In this case, you can make a
script that automates the process. Is it with this value
that we come to the password to the next level? Let's

test it step by step. Step by step We connected to HackersLab and found the encrypted program. Let's guess it now with the string chl1296rh which we got in the study where We tested encrypt thoroughly.We then run ./encrypt chl1296rh | more (to go to screen byscreen).Encryption will be applied a few dozen times and we will reach the encrypted result:

It's really the password we try to match the encrypted password that we were given. But does it work? Just testing to know ...That!!! The password works yes. This means that the password for level13 ischl1296rh.

9. Exploitation of Computer Systems

With the increase in the use of computer systems day by day, the percentage of attacks by third parties on the systems is also increasing gradually. There were days when people used to store all their data and confidential information in the form of physical copies. But, today most of the people prefer their confidential information in the computer systems and that is what gave birth to the attacks on computer systems. Exploitation is nothing but a programmed script or software which allows hackers to gain control over the entire system and then exploit the same for the benefit of the hackers.

The exploitation attacks try to take advantage of any form of weakness in an OS of the user, in the application or in any other form of software code that also includes plug-ins of the applications or of the libraries of software. The owners of such codes issue a patch or fix in response. The system users or the users of the applications are completely responsible behind obtaining the patch. It can be downloaded from the developer of software which is readily available on the web or it can also be downloaded by the OS automatically or by the application that needs the same. In case the user fails to install the required patch for a specific problem, it will expose the user to the exploitation of the computer system and might also lead to breaching of security.

Computer exploits and its types

Computer exploits can be categorized into two different types:

- *Remote exploits:* Remote exploits are those exploits types where it is not possible to access a network or remote system. Such exploits are generally used for gaining access to the systems which are remote in nature.

- *Local exploits:* Local exploits are used for those systems which are having local system access. The attackers use this for over-passing the rights of the users of the local systems.

The security exploits can come in all forms of size and shape. However, there are certain techniques among the lot which are more often used than the others. The most common vulnerabilities which are web-based are

XSS or cross-site scripting, SQL injection along with cross-site request forgery. It also includes abuse of authentication codes which are broken in nature or other misconfigurations of system security.

Zero-day exploit

The exploits of computer systems can be differentiated in various ways that will depend on the process of working of the exploits along with the attack type that it can accomplish. The most common form of exploit is zero-day exploit. This form of exploit takes ultimate advantage of the zero-day susceptibility. Zero-day susceptibility takes place when a software that might also be an application or an OS, consists of some critical form of vulnerability in the security measures that the vendor is also unaware of. The system vulnerability can only be detected when any hacker is detected with exploiting the susceptibility of the system. That is why it is known as zero-day exploit. After such an exploit takes place, the system which is running the software is also left vulnerable to all forms of attacks until and unless the software vendor releases the required patch for the correction of the system vulnerability.

The computer exploits can also be characterized according to the expected form of an attack like the execution of remote code, delivery of malware, escalation of privilege, denial of service and various other harmful goals. The exploits can be characterized according to the vulnerability type which is being exploited that also includes code injection, exploits of buffer overflow and various other attacks of side channel and vulnerabilities of input validation.

How does exploit take place?

It is a fact that exploits can take place in various ways. However, one of the most common methods of all is exploits being launched from the websites which are malicious in nature. The victim of such exploits generally visits the malicious websites by mistake. The victim might also be tricked into surfing or clicking on a malicious site link that can come attached with a phishing mail or in the form of advertisement of malicious nature.

The malicious websites which are being used for the computer exploits come equipped with various toolkits of software and exploit packs which can be used easily for unleashing the attacks against the various vulnerabilities of the browser right from a harmful website. It might also be from a hacked website. Such form of attack generally attacks the software which is coded in JAVA, browser plug-ins and the browsers which are unpatched. It is used for planting malware into the computer system of the targeted victim.

The automated form of exploits which are generally launched by various malicious websites are designed with two components: exploit code and shell code. Exploit code is a software which tries to exploit a known form of vulnerability. The payload of the exploiting software is the shell code which has been designed for running one single time when the breaching of the system is complete. The name of shell code comes from the very fact that many of the payloads open up command shell which is used for running the commands in opposition to the system of the target. However, all shell codes are not capable of opening a command shell.

Shell code

Shell code acts as a tiny piece of code which is used as the payload in the process of software exploitation. The shell codes are written in the form of machine codes. Download and execute is a form of shell code that performs by downloading and then executing some malware from directly on the targeted system. This form of shell code do not generate shell but instructs the target machine for downloading a form of an executable file which will be off the network, then save the same into the disk and execute the file. This form of shell code is most often used in drive download form of attack in which the victim clicks on a malicious website link and the shell code downloads the malware and installs the same on the system of the targeted victim.

10. How to Spoof Addresses

Macintosh address ridiculing is a system for incidentally changing your Media Access Control (MAC) address on a system gadget. A MAC Address is an interesting and hardcoded address customized into system gadgets which can't be changed forever. The MAC address is in the second OSI layer and ought to be viewed as the physical location of your interface. Macchanger is an instrument that is incorporated with any rendition of Kali Linux including the 2016 moving release and can change the MAC address to any ideal location until the following reboot. In this instructional exercise we will parody the MAC address of our remote connector with an irregular MAC address created by Macchanger on Kali Linux.

➤First we have to bring down the system connector so as to change the MAC address. This should be possible utilizing the accompanying direction: The ifconfig instrument will be supplanted by iproute2. Utilize the accompanying direction to bring down wlan1 with iproute2:

➤   Replace wlan1 with your own system interface.

➤ Now utilize the accompanying direction to change your MAC address to another irregular MAC Address:

➤ As appeared on the screen capture, Macchanger will demonstrate to you the perpetual, current and changed MAC address. The lasting MAC Address will be reestablished to your system connector after a reboot or you can reset your system connectors MAC address physically. Utilize the accompanying direction to reestablish the perpetual MAC address to your system connector physically:

➤ You can likewise parody a specific MAC address utilizing the accompanying direction: ifconfig wlan1 up

➤ Or utilize the accompanying iproute2 direction to bring the wlan1 gadget back up: ip connection set wlan1 up

A developing position of Internet hooligans are currently utilizing new deceives called "phishing" and "ridiculing" to take your personality. Sham messages that endeavor to fool clients into giving out close to home data are the most sizzling new trick on the Internet.

"Parodying" or "phishing" cheats endeavor to cause web clients to accept that they are getting email from a particular, confided in source, or that they are safely associated with a believed site, when that is not the situation by any stretch of the imagination, a long way from it. Mocking is commonly utilized as a way to persuade people to reveal individual or money related data which empowers the culprits to submit charge card/bank extortion or different types of wholesale fraud.

➤ In "email ridiculing" the header of an email seems to start from somebody or some place other than the genuine source. Spam merchants frequently use email mocking trying to get their beneficiaries to open the message and perhaps even react to their sales.

"IP ridiculing" is a system used to increase unapproved access to PCs. In this example the deceitful interloper makes an impression on a PC with an IP address showing that the message is originating from a confided in source.

"Connection change" includes the modifying of an arrival web address of a page that is messaged to a shopper so as to divert the beneficiary to a programmer's website as opposed to the authentic webpage. This is cultivated by including the programmer's IP address before the genuine location in an email which has a solicitation returning to the first site. On the off chance that an individual accidentally gets a satirize email and continues to "click here to refresh" account data, for instance, and is diverted to a site that looks precisely like a business site, for example, eBay or PayPal, there is a decent shot that the individual will finish in submitting individual as well as credit data. Furthermore, that is actually what the programmer is relying on.

The most effective method to Protect Yourself

· If you have to refresh your data on the web, utilize a similar strategy you've utilized previously, or open another program window and type in the site address of the genuine organization's page.

· If a site's location is new, it's likely not real. Just utilize the location that you've utilized previously, or even better, begin at the typical landing page.

· Most organizations expect you to sign in to a protected site. Search for the lock at the base of your program and "https" before the site address.

· If you experience a spontaneous email that demands, either straightforwardly or through a site, for individual budgetary or personality data, for example, Social Security number, passwords, or different identifiers, practice outrageous alert.

· Take note of the header address on the site. Most real locales will have a generally short web address that typically delineates the business name pursued by ".com," or potentially ".organization." Spoof destinations are bound to have an exorbitantly long solid of characters in the header, with the real business name some place in the string, or perhaps not in the least.

· If you have any questions about an email or site, contact the real organization legitimately. Make a duplicate of the flawed site's URL address, send it to the genuine business and inquire as to whether the solicitation is authentic

How computerize undertakings

For the individuals who don't have the foggiest idea how full scale programming computerizes undertakings, or whether they even have large scale programming, the basic answer is that you perused this book and after that you have a total comprehension of how full scale programming robotizing assignments.

Keeping an eye on similar locales, recollecting passwords, submitting to look through architects, just as testing sites again and again are the dreary undertakings for each internet browser ordinary. What's more, filling structures, running projects at a specific time, messing around, just as planning errands consistently are dull redundancy. Your undertaking can be any of those monotonous assignments. On the off chance that at least one of these assignments are happening each day, mechanizing these monotonous undertakings will assist you with saving your valuable time and to improve efficiency.

There are two fundamental approaches to computerize dull assignments - record keystroke and mouse exercises or alter content physically with full scale programming. Both of the ways can be spared as a full scale and later it would be replayed by utilizing any of these strategies - hotkey, scheduler and trigger. Clearly, attempted these errands by chronicle keystroke and mouse exercises is a basic way. Nonetheless, the way can not finish those unpredictable assignments except if the undertakings are finished just by utilizing keystroke and mouse exercises, for example, clicking catches on a window. So for those mind boggling errands, there is an a lot simpler and faster way - alter content physically.

To start utilizing along these lines, you should comprehend what content manager is in large scale programming. Large scale content manager is a device for altering full scale activities. Albeit a large scale can be made by account, in any case, the chronicle just catches the mouse and the console exercises. In this manner, for getting other complex activities, for example, sitting tight for a window centered, you can utilize content editorial manager worked in large scale programming to alter these activities and computerize to execute them later.

By utilizing thusly, you can computerize any arrangement of undertakings on your PC, running from just individual errands, to complex business assignments and significantly more. Simultaneously, you can utilize large scale programming to effectively make the errands: browsing email, moving or support up documents, sending email, and progressively complex computerization, including restrictive IF/ELSE explanations, circles, factors and other propelled alternatives.

Presently, you have realized how large-scale programming robotizes assignments. In the event that you have no one, you have to either download a free or preliminary duplicate from the web, or buy a duplicate of your picked programming.

158

11. FAQs

How often should penetration testing be done?

The organizations perform according to their own set of regulations and mandates. The standard that they follow will determine whether they need penetration testing or not. The standards of the organizations come with their own methodologies that help in describing what will be the best practice for protecting the security system. The standard will also determine that whether documentation of the tests needs to be done for compliance and purpose of auditing afterwards.

What is the rogue wireless network?

Rogue wireless network acts simply as a point of access just like a router or Wi-Fi station. It is plugged into the network of the organization; however, it does not even adhere to with the organization's standards for the wireless infrastructure which is in existence.

How a rogue wireless network can be installed?

This form of security threat occurs when any device has been adapted in an organization and is connected with the network, either knowingly or unknowingly. There are various types of equipment that come with activated Wi-Fi by default which is not configured at all. This means, that when the device gets turned on for the first time, it will start broadcasting signal for connection.

Can the employees of a business expose the organization to cyber threats?

Yes, they can. Any person who carries a device that has a connection with the Wi-Fi of the company might turn out to be a potential threat for the business. Malware can get into a system unknowingly via a network through laptop, tablet or smartphones. It happens when the segments of Wi-Fi are not properly locked. If the business servers are not separated on a completely different VLAN and all wireless network traffic can access the same, there is a high chance of security breaching and data theft.

Is it required to have wireless networks for businesses in spite of the associated potential risks?

Modern businesses cannot function without wireless technologies. However, the standards of technology and configuration which are applied for the wireless equipment will determine the usefulness of the wireless technologies and also the potential risks of security breach. There are various forms of businesses where the employees are required to work with tablets and scanners, especially in the manufacturing and warehousing sector. It will not be possible for such businesses to operate without the presence of a wireless network within the organization.

What are the most common types of Wi-Fi attacks?

When it comes to Wi-Fi attacks, the list is never-ending. There are several vulnerabilities, exploits and shortfall of security when it is related to wireless attacks. But, the attackers employ certain common methods for the purpose of accessing the wireless networks.

Is MITM a serious security threat?

Also known as man in the middle, it is one of the most commonly found forms of attack and is the most used tactic as well by the attackers. The attacker tricks the victim and transmits data so that the sufferer believes that the communication is coming from a legitimate form of contact only. Using MITM, the attackers can easily target the system of the victim and control it remotely, gain access to several sensitive data such as bank details along with exploits.

What are packet analyzers?

The attackers are capable of analyzing and sniffing the data packets which are being transported through a wireless network. The attackers can also intercept various unencrypted data which is inside the packets of TCP as well. When data is gathered using this method, the attackers can easily gain insight into the internal working system of an organization which is being targeted and can also fish out valuable information that might turn out to be a huge loss for the business.

What is malware?

Malware is a form of cyber attack and is the most common form of attacks. It possesses a serious kind of threat to the networks and servers. It also comes with the power of self-propagating over various networks. It becomes very difficult to detect and stop it once it has gained access to a network segment. It can infect the system when two devices are being connected with the same network which makes the spread of infection very fast.

Can poorly configured Wi-Fi lead to cyber attack?

Yes, it is possible when the Wi-Fi is configured poorly. It is the main reason behind the infiltration of a wireless network. This becomes more serious when there are no available management tools for the IT staffs to gain a perspective of the wireless environment.

Is it okay to share the result of penetration test outside the organization?

No, you should never disclose the test report outside the organization. You can only share it with the company officials and authorities. Sharing test results with the outside world will open up vulnerabilities for the organization and might lead to a serious cyber attack.

Conclusion

Congratulations! You've come a long way since you first opened this book! It might've been difficult but progressing through the cyber-security field can be extremely rewarding and satisfying. You should not be ready to start with penetration testing on your own without the training wheels. You will become a professional ethical hacker in no time if you put the work into it.

The journey is not over yet, however. Don't rely on this content alone, because penetration testing is such a developed topic that you can write entire bookcases on it. This guide should clear up the mystery behind ethical hacking and guide you through all the basic penetration testing methods, however reading a book is not enough. You must take action! Develop your skills further by taking advantage of all the online resources on hacking and join a community with the same interests as you.

With that message in mind, let's go briefly through everything you gained by reading this book:

It's important to understand basic terminology and what a penetration test actually is. We also spent some time exploring the mind of the black hat hacker, because as an ethical hacker you will have to walk in his shoes sometimes in order to create accurate simulations of a real attack. Do not take unnecessary risks, and always perform a test only if you are fully authorized to do so.

www.ingramcontent.com/pod-product-compliance
Lightning Source LLC
LaVergne TN
LVHW052100060326
832903LV00060B/2447